HEALING THE FAMILY HEART HOLES

A Genealogical Quest to Solve an Illegal Adoption Mystery Using DNA, Old Records, and Irish Luck

by: Robin Gerry

D1409950

ISBN: 9781795726313 (paperback)

On the Cover: Barbara Katherine Gray, the author's mother, Circa 1938–40

DEDICATION

This book is dedicated to my great country,
The United States of America.
Thank you for taking in and welcoming
my impoverished, traumatized, desperate
and hard-working ancestors
who were fleeing hunger, violence and oppression.
Thank you for giving these poor immigrants the
opportunity to become loyal Americans.

Should auld acquaintance be forgot,
and never brought to mind?
Should auld acquaintance be forgot
and auld lang syne?
For auld lang syne my dear,
for auld lang syne.
We'll take a cup o' kindness yet,
for auld lang syne.

– Robert Burns, 1788

CONTENTS

1

THE DESPERATE SEARCH BEGINS AND THE HEART HOLE IS PASSED ON

BARBARA IS ON THE TELEPHONE.

"Aunt Nellie, it's me, Barbara. Barbara your niece. Don't you remember me? Jenny's little girl. Your sister Jennie. Jennie. Jennie. Do you remember Jennie?

You used to babysit me. Yeah … Barbara. Barbara, your niece.

I'm calling because I'm trying to find my birth parents. I hoped you would remember something, anything, from my adoption … Barbara. Your niece, Barbara.

Remember my adopted brother, Donald? You used to babysit us.

Remember the time we were floating down the river on an iceberg

1

outside your office? While you were supposed to be watching us? Remember how scared you were and how you had to get the town folk to rescue us? Remember?

It's me, Barbara. I'm grown up now. I'm in my 50s. I'm your niece, remember? Jennie's daughter. Your sister, Jennie …

Oh, Aunt Nellie, please try to remember. You're the only elder left. Please try to remember. Please…"

Aunt Nellie was born in 1878. It is the mid-1970s now, and Nellie is nearly 100 years old. And she wasn't having a good memory day.

"Yes, it is sunny today, Aunt Nellie. You're tired? Okay. I understand. I'll try to call you tomorrow. Maybe tomorrow you will remember me? Your niece… Barbara. Barbara Gray."

My mother hung up the phone, and I watched her slump onto the step to the bathroom. It was the only place to sit and still be able to talk on the black, boxy, shiny wall phone with the three-foot cord. The fact that my father chose to put the only phone in the house between two bathrooms was evidence of his limited understanding of what it meant to be a human on this planet – or at least a limited understanding of what it should have meant to live with three daughters and a wife. No one in the house ever had the sort of privacy we wanted and needed for all sorts of business.

That day, though, the twisted phone cord somehow seemed like an umbilical connection to a fading dream.

Her cheeks were red, and her eyes were teary. Seeing my mother get misty like that was a completely unnerving experience for me. She was not a crier. Ever. No matter what. Not when my sisters and I broke bones, not when we got sick, not when we got bitten by dogs. Never ever.

In fact, until then, I had only ever seen her cry once in my life. It happened during a family dinner. My mother was never much of a cook, but she tried to be creative. This was the era of white Wonder Bread building strong bones and strong bodies in twelve different ways, and of believing that real white rice only takes sixty seconds to cook. Our house had two spices – salt and pepper. And it wasn't until I was in college that I realized *Velveeta* wasn't really cheese but a processed cheese product. I still don't really know what that even means. Despite her pedestrian culinary skills, dinners were still important to her. She tried hard to make the meals nice and have us all sit together. Meals were always scheduled around my dad's job and gastric preferences. He worked rotating shifts and was always sleeping, sleepy or just plain exhausted. Nonetheless, meal times were family times.

On the day I saw her cry, she had made her famous meat loaf. She was always proud of her meatloaf although looking back, I realize now that it wasn't that complicated or even much to brag about. She would just throw in a package of dried onion soup mix into ground beef and call it a day. She probably got that culinary trick from one of the women's magazines on the counter at the grocery store check-out line. As a bonus though, she would hide one or two hard boiled eggs inside the meatloaf for my sisters, Billie and Dawn, and me to try finding. Oddly, that was always a fun treat for us when we were young.

Anyway, one evening the meatloaf didn't cut into slices. It just kept crumbling into small, little, lumpy pieces. That was a first as it usually held together in a gluey way by an insane amount of fat and grease. My father, always the carver, tried mightily to cut it into neat, square pieces. It wasn't working. In the end, he became untypically frustrated with such a stupid thing and began angrily scooping up crumbly meatloaf nuggets with his hands and flinging them onto our plates. This was unlike him. My mother was initially silent but then began to cry. She then ran off into their bedroom. I can't recall ever seeing my parents fight before, so her crying and him flinging meatloaf around certainly seemed apocalyptic. My father stomped to the sink to wash the meatloaf grease off his hands, barked at us kids to finish our meal. He then followed my mother into the bedroom. Armageddon had to be close at hand for sure.

My sisters, Billie and Dawn, and I, in the way that children tend to think, were trying to figure out what we should do. Like any of that had anything to do with us. Yet as kids tend to do, we felt oddly responsible.

In the end though, we wound up eating the meatloaf with our hands too, as our father had sort of set a precedent for that day. The sneakiness of that bold act of defiance among us three sisters seemed to mark us as savage girls. Honestly, it was thrilling to be so primal on the down low.

The meatloaf catastrophe had occurred while we were in elementary school, so it had been years and years since I'd seen my mother as upset as she was on the phone call with poor, sweet, senile old Aunt Nellie. While my mother was on the phone trying to bring her aunt back into a world with a semblance of a reality, where she could possibly reconnect with her aunt and maybe get help with an orphan's desperate need, I was standing in the doorway of the next room, immobile and transfixed.

I was as stunned as those gazelles in the Serengeti get when the cheetah is about to leap on them and eat a leg off. My mother didn't realize I was there until she finally looked up from her despair and saw me standing there still frozen and befuddled.

"What do you want?" she asked in the best cranky voice she could muster up as she wiped her eyes and ran a hand through her short, salt and pepper hair. Looking back, I now see that she may have felt humiliated or somehow too vulnerable. On those rare occasions when she had inadvertently allowed someone to witness her humanity, perhaps it seemed somehow shameful to her? Maybe? I'm not really sure. I do know, though, that she struggled to tolerate, express and trust her emotions until her dying breath. It had a tremendous impact on her life, but that's another story.

Or is it?

This is the story of her biological parents. Maybe it is really the same story? Now that I am writing this, it is totally clear to me that her feelings, thoughts and behaviors were inextricably linked to the sad gaps in her life story. How could her feelings and emotions not be the movie stars of her own life story? How could they not shape the choices she would make? Boy, they sure did have an impact, in both amazingly wonderful and devastating ways.

Anyway, back to my frozen befuddlement. I was close to being a teenager, and totally oblivious to my own immaturity and ignorance. Not out of disrespect, but likely more out of confusion and a desire to protect my mother from a person who could wound her like this, I demanded of her, "Who was that? What were you talking about?"

She was unexpectedly frank with me, another bit of end-times foreboding for me that day. She went into a long explanation about how Aunt Nellie was her last, living adoptive relative and how she was feeling desperate (a word she never, ever used) to find out who her birth parents were and what was the true circumstance of her informal adoption. She told me it was something that had bothered her all of her life, and now she just wanted to know, needed to know, who her birth parents were and why they didn't raise her. She explained that it was something that was sometimes tormenting to her.

Tormenting. That is a huge word. She never spoke like that. Ever.

When she saw the look on my face, she tried to soothe my worry for her and explained that she had a good life and her need to know had nothing to do with her adoptive home. She said she felt grateful to her adoptive parents. It was something more primal than that.

She wondered if she had biological siblings. Were any of them alive? Were there nieces and nephews? Cousins? She wondered about family. Her family. She said she couldn't explain why, but it felt like "an old hole in my heart that never healed."

A heart hole...

Silence.

More silence.

Silence for a thousand years.

We stared at each other. She had never talked to me like that before ... and never since. I was vaguely aware that this was some sort of huge moment. A gift maybe? Or perhaps something just really unusual for her? The tectonic plates of my emotional earth felt like they had somehow shifted, but I couldn't quite tell where the earthquake was or if there was even an earthquake or a new fault line. Certainly, her emotional earth erupted that day too, at least a little bit. Her magma was oddly cold and frozen though. If this was a gift, I certainly was not mature enough to appreciate it or know how to respond to that at my young age.

In all my preadolescent wisdom and bravado, I said, "What do you even care about that now for? You're so old and have lived so long. Besides, you have us. What more do you need from your life?"

She was quiet. Then she said, "Yeah. You're right." And she walked away. She walked to a place that I couldn't follow. An orphan place. A place I couldn't see. A place I couldn't understand. A place where even a daughter couldn't walk with a mother. A dark place where one can only walk alone.

Looking back at that moment with my mother, a moment that's been frozen in my memory for decades, I cringe with horror at how utterly inadequate and unkind my adolescent, narcissistic response was to her raw, emotional wounds and pain. This conversation was well beyond my maturity and intelligence. At the time though, I thought I had really calmed her down. Ahh...the omnipotence of youth. I was too immature to even realize how insensitive I was. I feel so ashamed now about how I responded to her then, that I had even considered not sharing it and not putting it into this book as it is extremely embarrassing and distressing for me at this point in my life. But, as I am telling her truth, I know I need to share my own truth, too.

I didn't realize it then, but that the sacred moment between my mother and me had stamped my heart forever, too. It would take decades for me to understand that not knowing who your people are or where you come from can create a hole in the heart – one that can be passed on to the next generation. It wasn't until I

was in my 50s – the age my mother was when she made that call
to her Aunt Nellie – that I realized her heart hole had somehow
become a heart hole for me, too.

How on earth did that happen?

My mother died without ever finding her family. She never
learned what her ethnicity was. She never learned what medi-
cal problems ran in the family and what to look out for. She
wound up dying of colon cancer. If she had known something,
anything about her family, maybe that could have been pre-
vented? She was gone long before the advent of DNA genealogical testing. Throughout this process, I kept trying to imagine
what she would think and feel to be living in these times. These
miraculous times when dark secrets are brought to light with
just a little spit.

She died before she could have legitimately had an honest hope,
and a reasonable dream to finally find the identity of her biological parents and learn the truth about why they didn't raise her.
If she had been able to get the answers to her lifelong tormenting wonder, would she have even had the heart hole? How would
that have changed her life? Her choices? Would I even be here if
things had been different for her?

I am a big believer that things turn out the way they need to in
the end. But it's still difficult to not get bogged down with all of
the 'What ifs?'

This book is the story of a daughter hoping to finish a mother's
quest, one that couldn't really ever go beyond that tentative phone
call to a sweet, old woman with dementia. In the process, perhaps
I was also trying to find redemption for myself and maybe fix my
own heart hole?

In this search for her truth, I found an utterly unbelievable and impossible story of brilliance, despicable acts, fame, good old Irish survival and German ingenuity. There is an honest-to-God princess, Irish kings, a scoundrel, some movie stars, an accusation of Islamic terrorism and an Irish bog man. There is utter rejection from some of the family but mostly an incredible, open-armed welcome from other new family members.

In short, this is the story of my heart's journey.

2

THE ILLEGAL BABY GIVE-AWAY

No one really knows the circumstances of my mother's birth and adoption. It was likely illegal and shady.

The family story goes that, without a birth certificate or adoption papers, my mother was somehow just handed over to her 'adoptive' parents, Solomon Hotchkiss Gray and Jennie Butler Gray, maybe sometime during the winter of 1921. My mother did not even legally exist as anyone, but informally she became Barbara Katherine Gray. Did she come with the name Barbara Katherine? Or did the Grays name her? Who knows?

This secret and undocumented act would prove to be a significant problem for her throughout her entire life. She would need Congressional intervention to join the Navy, get married, get a passport, get a Social Security card. Without a birth certificate, she was legally no one.

And Trump claims Obama had a "birther" problem?!

It seems likely that she was born around January or February of 1921. There is what appears to be a christening picture of her with her adoptive parents in the spring of 1921. She is looking pretty tiny in that picture.

She always celebrated her birthday on February 24, but there is no documentation verifying whether or not this was her actual birthday.

Jenny and Solomon Hotchkiss Gray with their adopted baby
Barbara circa May 1921.
(Don't the Grays remind you a little bit of that painting
'American Gothic' by Grant Wood?)

The Grays had apparently lost one baby, then had trouble conceiving or carrying another one to full term. My mother's older adoptive cousin, Elsie Winterberger, had written letters detailing how sweet Jennie Gray was with family children. Jennie would host parties for children in the extended family even before she had any kids of her own, adopted or otherwise. She just loved the wee ones. She was a school teacher and always seemed to want to be near children. There's a lovely story about Jennie dressing up as Santa for Elsie's first-grade class and walking Elsie home from school afterwards. Elsie said she felt so special and chosen to be picked by the real Santa Claus for such an honor. Elsie eventually wound up being the town historian for Fallsburg, New York and actually wrote about that episode in a Fallsburg newspaper article.

Jennie Gray was a woman just dying to be a mother. And would do anything to be a mother.

About three years before my mother was placed with the Grays, the couple had adopted a baby boy and named him Donald. Although that adoption was supposedly legal, Donald also never had a birth certificate. That is another of the mysteries in this book, why didn't he have a birth certificate either? In those days though, a baptismal certificate apparently sufficed as documentation, and he did have a baptismal certificate- from the Grays.

My uncle eventually learned from Elsie that he had been a WWI "Nellie Bly baby."

Nellie Bly was a fascinating, charismatic, bright and socially forward – thinking woman who lived in the New York City/Long Island area. During World War I, she began to bring orphaned babies born to European women and U.S. soldiers back to the United States from Europe. Then she helped arrange for their adoptions.

The Grays lived a couple of counties up from New York City in Sullivan County, New York. It is likely that they found out about Nellie Bly through advertisements in local newspapers. The presumption is that the Gray's were looking for a baby to adopt and chose that venue. It's not known why they didn't or wouldn't go to one of the many foundling homes in New York City to adopt him.

According to family lore, Donald's German mother died in childbirth and his American soldier father died soon after in combat. A German and an American? It always seemed a little odd to me that they died so close together. I think it was maybe a little unbelievable to my Uncle Donald, too? Letters written between us in his later years suggest that he was still actively searching for the details of his birth family when he was well into his late sixties.

Is the need to know who our people are maybe just a deep primal thing? Almost an instinct? Like feeling wonder at the night sky? Or being afraid of the dark? Both my mother and my uncle seemed to feel this yearning and need. Both felt the torment of feeling adrift from their own personal histories and their biological families. I think that their wondering maybe impacted the people they became. Possibly tormented them a little? Maybe it's not such a bad thing though as they both turned out to be good, decent humans.

I consider myself a bit of a Nellie Bly expert now. I did a lot of research on her in an effort to find her records of the adoptions and newspaper advertisements about the available babies. I was hoping to find a direction to go toward understanding the circumstances of my mother's birth and adoption. I had no success in getting a list of the babies Nellie brokered. I was looking for a clue to start to figure out my mother's story. Any kind of clue. I was hoping that there might be a list of babies; maybe not their names, but perhaps their birthdays? My thinking was that I would then cross reference things to try to deduce which baby was my mother. It was a fool's quest. I would come to realize during this search that there were many more dead ends than real leads. It's certainly a reality that I didn't understand when I started this search. Rejection, false hope and genealogical stone walls would come to be constant companions for me in this journey. It was honestly quite humbling.

I did find a lot of information online about Nellie Bly's journalism career though. She was a very hands-on reporter. In fact, she even once had herself admitted to a mental hospital in order to report on conditions there. She enjoyed a great deal of fame for her work, and she became a journalism celebrity in her own right. She certainly helped make the world a better place.

Here is where the story becomes peculiar to me, though – one of the many mysteries in this book. The Grays knew Nellie Bly and had allegedly gotten my uncle from her. Wouldn't you think that they'd go back to Nellie for a second baby? True, the World War I ended in 1918, a few years before my mother was born. So maybe Nellie was done with the adoption business by then? If so, wouldn't it be likely that she'd still have some connections in the business? And maybe knew somebody who knew somebody who knew about an available baby? Or maybe they did contact Nellie and Nellie just couldn't help them again. Who knows?

Nellie Bly operated above board, even if there were no formal adoption papers for my uncle.

The adoption process involving my mother was shady and dark from the start.

There are three conflicting stories forming the basis of what little my mother knew of her 'adoption.' I use the A word loosely.

One was that my mother's mother was a teenager who had died during childbirth. In that version, my great grandmother then just handed the baby over to the Grays. To my sisters and I, we envisioned a dark alley where fumbling hands grab for a baby held tight to someone's chest. Very shady and very scary. Very dark. How would an agreement like that have ever gotten brokered in the first place? How would the Grays even have heard of an available baby? Why did they agree to such a below-board arrangement?

As I write this, though, I realize that people often do anything to get a child, so I actually know the answer to that question – the Gray's would have agreed to any terms.

Jennie Gray's niece Elsie wrote in a letter years after my mother died (and Elsie was nearing eighty), that she remembered hearing that "Barbara, as a newborn baby, was placed in Aunt Jennie's arms in the Foundling Home by Barbara's maternal grandmother. The grandmother told Aunt Jennie, 'Don't ever try to get in touch with the family because only I know this child was born.'" Elsie remembered that the grandmother had a Russian last name, but she couldn't recall it. Elsie thought that the baby's first name was Rachel at birth.

That's a pretty rough start for a little baby, isn't it?

A second story holds that my mother was very sickly when she was born and wound up in a Catholic orphanage in New York City. The dead mother thing sort of coincides with the first part of the story. Apparently when the Grays came looking for a baby, the nuns asked them if they would take our mother home with them, as she was so sickly and so tiny that no one expected her to live for very long. The nuns felt that such a little soul deserved to die in a proper home with proper parents before she met her maker. There were so many children and babies in the orphanage that the nuns didn't have the time or ability to properly care for a sickly newborn. The Grays then could come back for a "good" baby after my mother died.

According to this story, the baby went home with the Grays that day. Allegedly Jennie stayed with the baby night and day and slowly loved my mom back to health. It was supposedly one of Jennie's proudest accomplishments.

The trouble with this story is, what were a couple of Protestants doing in a Catholic orphanage? Would the nuns even have released a baby to non-Catholics? Without papers? Maybe? But probably the New York Foundling Hospital adoptions would have been legit.

My mother's adoption was totally illegal.

The third story is that my mother's biological mother was an Irish actress of some renown in the silent movie era, and that her biological father was a Russian sculptor. That sounded cool. Very cool.

In fact, the movie star story is the one my sisters and I adopted as the truest. After very careful childhood evaluation and assessment, we finally narrowed it down to either Lucille Ball or Maureen O'Hara as our Irish actress grandmother. The age impossibilities of that hypothesis were irrelevant to us. We had no clue how old they were anyway. We needed a grandmother, and who wouldn't want Lucy and Ricky as grandparents? This version of my mother's background – embellished by us kids over the years – was so much a part of the background music of our child-hood, that one of my sisters honestly believed that Lucille Ball was really our grandmother until she was in her fifties. Adding to our childhood evidence was the fact that both she and Lucy were redheads. See??? Right there is proof enough for children. Plus, my sisters both had freckles. It seemed that Lucille Ball may not have had freckles, but we explained that away as Hollywood make-up tricks.

Everyone else Loved Lucy, but my sisters and I *honestly, sincerely and wholeheartedly Loved Lucy!* We loved her deep to the very bottom of our childish, yearning, naive hearts. For ever and ever. Who wouldn't love their own grandmother? Especially one as funny as Lucy. How lucky were we?

Supposedly my mother's hair was a dark auburn well into her adulthood, but who really knows about the color of her hair in childhood? The photo prints from that period are sepia, so it's hard to tell what color her hair really was. It seemed light, though. Maybe strawberry blond? We knew her only with salt and pepper hair, but when she was a kid? Anything was possible.

Maureen O'Hara would have been a very close second for our vote for grandmother. She was beautiful and such a bad ass with John Wayne in *The Quiet Man*. We were actually kind of uncom-fortable though with how mean she was to him in the movie, but we were so desperate for a grandmother that we looked past that. We were creating our own story of our history, our own little opus. That weird right? Who does that? The movie star theory was certainly the one with the most glitz and glam.

I would eventually learn that our biological grandfather was sort of, kind of in the movie business. Not exactly, really, but he worked for Adolf Zuker, the guy who started Paramount Pictures.

Zuker was a prominent player in the silent movie era. Among other things, my grandfather helped build Zuker's yacht, then he was the ship's captain once it was afloat. Before that he was a chauffeur; possibly for Zuker? He was around famous actresses all the time. How crazy is that? Could the Irish actress thing really be true? More about that later.

I am so struck now by how odd and desperate it was that my sisters and I worked so hard as children to conjure a grandmother. Is that even normal? If the three of us were so taken with the missing grandmother story and we were a generation removed from it, what was it even like for our mother?

Maybe all three stories had an element of truth? Or maybe they were all blarney? Jennie died with the secret. Obviously, there are problems with all of the theories. If my mother had, indeed, been plucked out of a Catholic orphanage, there likely would have been some adoption or birth records. The whole "hand the baby over to strangers in the street" theory is pretty unbelievable and horrifying, but it could explain the lack of papers. How would the Grays even have known about the baby, though? It sort of sounds like televisions falling off the back of a truck. Very shady.

What was the connection between the Grays – a teacher and carpenter in Sullivan County, New York – to an out-of-wedlock baby born in New York City? Not that we were really sure she actually *had* been born in the city. Was this just another erroneous presumption? See how easy it is to absorb family stories as truth? None of it really made much sense. Maybe the Grays had legitimate adoption papers but just never gave them to my mother?

In Elsie's letter to Uncle Donald during the period when he was desperately searching for his own biological parents, she confirmed that he was a Nellie Bly baby – but that my mother wasn't. She said that her Aunt Jennie was always terrified that my mother's biological mother would someday come back and just take the baby back. It's always the mother that was mentioned, never the father. Why is that? Why do these kinds of stories always seem to focus mostly on the mother? Besides, wasn't the mother supposed to be dead?

Jennie's fear that the mother or biological grandmother would return and claim baby Barbara suggests they may have known each other. How? It's another of the primary mysteries of this story.

Maybe all three stories hold an element of truth. Or maybe they're all blarney. Jennie would die with the secret.

Naturally there was a deathbed scene during which the subject came up – a story my mother told us years later.

Jennie and Solomon Gray apparently never told their daughter anything about the biological mother. Or father. Maybe they didn't know anything about the father? According to my mother, Jennie, on her deathbed, asked my mother if she wanted to know the true identity of her biological mother. This deathbed offer of the truth came as a complete surprise as both my mother and Uncle Donald indicated that Jennie was a very secretive woman – a woman who didn't even tell her two children they were adopted until they were teenagers. Divulging secrets was not an easy thing for Jennie Gray.

But on her deathbed, according to my mother, Jennie again said that her biological mother was an actress of some renown and had even recently been on television. Jennie offered to reveal the name. As a final gift to her dying adoptive mother, my own mother replied, "No, I don't need to know that. You're the only mother I've ever had and the only one I will ever care about." On May 1, 1953, Jennie then died with the the secret. *The secret.* The secret that would change all of our lives.

An adopted daughter's last gift to her beloved dying mother.

And my mother's cootie curse to me.

I suspect it was a *gift* that haunted my mother for the rest of her days.

These were the only "facts" that I had when I started this quest – nothing that even remotely offered any real clarity or direction. Nothing that even seemed realistic. Movie stars? Death bed confessions? Russian sculptors? Babies that were near death? Illegal baby hand off? How could one even expect to figure out a mystery with so many holes and inconsistencies? If nothing else, at least the story promised to maybe be a wild ride. It sure was.

To be honest, I never really did think that I'd actually be able to work this all through. My plan was to try to do something, anything, and then kiss it up to God. Maybe just to be able to say that I tried? Even that's odd to me now, my own motivation to take on this quest was as nebulous as all of these crazy stories.

I didn't realize when I started this that I was trying to fill heart holes. I didn't understand that there were three more little heart holes besides my mom's heart hole. It's an adoption thing, I guess.

3

A MISPLACED CHILDHOOD

As I was never told much about our mother's childhood, there isn't much to tell. Sadly. Very sadly.

That's sad but also odd. Why weren't there stories? Why did we never meet the Grays? Adopted aunts? Uncles? Cousins? My sisters and I had no sense of the Gray, Butler or Hotchkiss families. It's as though there were no connection; nothing my mother was either able and willing to share with us. Or share about us with them.

Through my research for this book, I discovered that the adoptive family is very large and close. Most don't live far from where I live now. I met Dan Hotchkiss online, a cousin from the Solomon Hotchkiss Gray side. Dan has to be the sweetest man ever. He told me they have huge family reunions. Cousins come in from all over the country. We never went to any of them or even heard about them. Why? Why was there such a disconnect from the adoptive family's extended family?

I was a small kid in the '60s, the years of the space race. I used to have nightmares about space walks and the astronauts becoming untethered and rolling through space toward infinity. Forever. That's sort of what it seems to me like it may have been for my mother? Untethered in space. Ungrounded, and just rolling on alone. Perhaps I am being dramatic? I don't know what it was really like for her because she never, ever talked about things like that. Did she feel that allowing these painful thoughts and questions to even form in her brain, would sort of be like conjuring up the fears and bringing the dark, frightened feelings to life? Like day time nightmare ghosts?

Through a series of career twists and coincidences, I wound up becoming a therapist in a child and adolescent sex abuse and trauma unit. I can't even tell you how many people tell me that they can't remember huge chunks of their childhood. This "forgetfulness" is almost always a response to trauma.

Was it a trauma response for my mother? It seemed as if she was always circling the event horizon of her life, never actually falling into the black hole but never getting back into the universe, either.

She was a dedicated mother who loved us all. And we knew we were loved. Yet she always seemed to struggle with openly showing love and affection to us. And with our father. I see this same struggle with attachment in many of the foster kids I work with. They can love people but learn not to get too close or show that they really care on an intimate, emotional level. Our mother was never an "I love you" kind of woman. She couldn't even put those words in writing until her later years.

I can't help but wonder if this emotional distance she put between herself and her family was due to some sort of trauma or drama in the adoptive family. I don't know.

But I do know that my mother never, ever spoke of her adopted father, Solomon. I don't know one story about him that I ever heard from her. I've heard a couple of Solomon snippets from a Gray grandson of Solomon's brother, but not much. He told me that Solomon was known to be grumpy, taciturn, distant and almost emotionally rude. On her military records, she crossed him off as her next of kin three times and chose her mother and brother instead. I don't know why. I can speculate, but in the end, the only two who know what – if anything – happened are long dead.

My mother spoke occasionally about her adopted mother Jennie, but not enough to give us a sense of who Jennie was. In a letter my mother wrote to me when I was an adult, she said her mother was the type who had to know *everything* at all times about her children and was quite an intrusive mother. My mother said that's why she tried not to interfere too much directly in our lives.

There were certainly times when she should have. But that's not this story.

I learned far more about Jennie through research for this book than I ever did from my mother. I remember hearing only three stories about Jennie. The biggest of those were of course the adoption story and the deathbed story.

The only other story I heard about was about Jennie's reaction when my mother decided to cut off every other of her banana curls. My mother remembered doing that because she understandably hated the pain of the daily hair torture to get the curls tight and bouncy. She did it thinking that Jennie wouldn't notice as there still seemed to be a lot of hair left. Jennie of course immediately noticed and apparently sobbed when she saw my mother's hair. That's it. Those are only stories I ever heard about Jenny. It was as if our mother had no personal history? Her childhood sort of seems to me like a child's drawing that eventually becomes so faded that the spark and glory disappear.

I know how trauma can create a hole in children. Forever. If she was unhappy in her adopted home, I have to think it could have had to increase her curiosity about her biological family. All kids occasionally wish for someone to show up on a white horse and save them. Heck, I used to wish my "real parents" would come and take me away when I got disciplined for something.

For a child who was being raised, possibly illegally, by a non-biological family, I have to wonder if the adoption issue became bigger for her whenever she was feeling unhappy.

Perhaps so. Perhaps not.

Barbara Katherine Gray and her banana curls at about age five circa 1926.

Did she feel unmoored? Untethered? Did the hole in her heart grow bigger? Or was it more like a virus that took aortic hold corpuscle by corpuscle, year after year? These things are so crucial in understanding my mother, but ultimately they are unknowable.

Did the growing intensity of her need in later years to know where and who she came from start in an unhappy childhood? Or was it just an adoption thing for her? Maybe both?

Another possibility that could explain her detachment from her extended adopted family could have been – embarrassment and shame.

My mother wound up enlisting in the Navy (more about that later). After she was discharged, she went home to Delaware County, New York. The Grays had moved there from Sullivan County. Delaware County was the next county further north. I always wondered if the move was an attempt to thwart the biological family from ever finding them. Was it a way to try to disappear? Or did Solomon just get a better job opportunity?

It was there in Delaware County that she wound up getting pregnant by her older, married boss.

She had the baby. And she gave the baby away. And she repeated the exact same cycle that damaged her own life so deeply. It still stuns me to this day.

Like her own biological family, she apparently knew where the baby was. After my mother died in 1990, my father casually and almost inadvertently mentioned that the only time she ever lied to him was when he caught her sneaking money to the child's adopted family, who were allegedly living in a western state. He said he never would have known had she not used the mortgage money.

I was stunned. I never had a clue that we had a half sibling.

We had a half sibling...

The news was like lightening to the heart. It was sort of what I imagine it must feel like when a doctor shocks an un-beating heart back into life. A major burst of raw, primal electricity that shakes the whole body and soul convulsively.

I have been trying to find my sibling ever since then. Ever since the second that I found out that I had a sibling, I've been looking for my sibling. Looking. Looking. I've been searching, writing letters, asking for records etc. I've been doing it off and on for over 25 years. Sadly though. I've been completely unsuccessful. I had no clue if my mother had a girl or a boy. Or what year they may have been born. Where they were born. Nothing. I have to admit that I was starting to worry a little that maybe my sibling would turn out to be a serial killer or pedophile or something? Maybe it was best if I didn't find them? I was pretty shocked at the level of my fears as well as my yearning to find my sibling.

It seems that the loss of my half sibling was another huge heart hole that my mother lived with every day. She obviously never forgot about or stopped wondering about and remembering the baby. She never stopped loving the baby. Lying and stealing were not parts of her character. She must have felt a desperate need, and sense of parental responsibility or connection to the baby, to still keep trying to support the child, in some way, from a distance. It is simultaneously touching and devastating.

When I started this quest, I was keener about finding that child – my half sibling, who might still be alive – rather than finding dead grandparents. I was quite sure that I had figured out where that baby landed. A sweet family. I made a few attempts to contact them. Initially, our communication was friendly and informative. But when I finally broached the subject of a missing sibling, they shut me down. I tried a couple more times to make contact but was shut down each time.

It really is a reality about this sort of quest, that one needs to be prepared for rejection. For myself, I would love if a horde of unknown siblings and relatives revealed themselves to me. It would be thrilling for our family. But other families feel differently. And that has to be ok. They're all not so into changing anything; even if the truth is at their doorstep.

I had promised myself when I started this quest that I would not interfere with anyone's life regardless of what I might discover during my research, so I accepted their choice to cut off communication. I had learned enough to know that my half sibling probably didn't know he or she was adopted. It seemed clear that others in the family were being protective.

I chose to leave it alone, but it's a choice that continues to haunt me.

And I still debate whether it was the right choice. I admit that, nearly every day, I check Ancestry.com to see if my half sibling has been tested. Every day, I hope he or she shows up near the top of the list. Every day, I am disappointed.

I understand the adopted family's desire to be protective, yet we are talking about an adult who should certainly have been told the truth by now. I am still in the process of letting that go.

Meanwhile, my focus has shifted back to my grandparents. They are the ones whose history I can research. They are the ones I can find, and finally learn the answers to my mother's life long searching and yearning for her story. Why was she given up? And why was it so shady and illegal?

It's my story now too now.

4

SEEKING A CULTURE

(Any Culture Will Do)

BARBARA MARRIED MY FATHER, BILL Gerry, sometime in the mid-1950s. We've never seen a marriage certificate, though. Did she have both an illegal adoption and marriage? Good Grief! Or did they just lose the marriage certificate? What are the odds of bad illegal paperwork lightning striking twice like this? I haven't bothered to try to find it. Be careful what you ask for seemed apropos to me for some odd reason. Secrets and mysteries seem to be one of the background themes of this family.

Apparently, they couldn't get married in New York state because a birth certificate was required before the marriage would be legal and legit and before anyone would even agree to even marry them. She was a decorated Navy veteran at the time she married. How could a veteran be treated like this? She couldn't even be married in her home state because of a missing piece of paper? I am sure that the adoptive and biological grandparents didn't really think about things like this when they agreed to whatever shady arrangement they came up with. Did they wonder how it would be for a child's mental and legal health to not be a legal person? Probably not. Who thought about children's mental health issues back then anyway?

Did my mother kind of feel like an alien mysteriously arriving in the night in a secret spaceship? In a world full of other children living legally with their parents. Maybe...

My parents wound up getting married in New Jersey instead, because apparently the regulations there were less stringent there at that time. Two friends served as witnesses, and they just went out to dinner afterwards. It doesn't sound like much of a celebration.

I remember driving through a highway with them somewhere as a teenager. My mother pointed out a bunch of buildings that simultaneously reminded her both of the place where the assassin who shot President Kennedy took aim, and also of the place where my parents got married. Good God! How could she even make as association like that with one thing that should have felt sacred and loving with the other thing that horrified and traumatized the entire country? Even then I remember thinking that was so sad.

They then had three girls – my sisters Dawn, Billie and me. I don't recall our parents ever celebrating their anniversary. It was an oddity that I didn't even realize was odd until I grew up and came to understand that most people want to celebrate their love on their wedding anniversary.

Was this seeming indifference to celebrating their anniversary because the state hadn't accepted her identity when she wanted to get married, thereby kind of throwing a pall over the whole event? Did the casual quality of the marriage ceremony somehow dilute her feelings about celebrating their anniversary? I believe it's just another instance of how this illegal baby give-away thing plagued her entire life.

Then there was her ethnic background. What was she? Where did her people come from What are *we*? Maybe Irish? My mother always said her hair was auburn. As she had given birth to us very late in her childbearing life, we only knew her as she was going gray.

My sister Billie has red hair and freckles. As a child, I would co-erce Billie into showing my friends her elbows and knees so they, too, could be amazed that she had freckles *everywhere!* My sister Dawn also has freckles, but they are not as bountiful as Billie's. I took after our British father. No freckles. We all have blue eyes. So maybe we're Irish?

As the Vikings raped and pillaged all over Ireland, Scotland, Wales and England, spreading redheads here, there and every-where, it certainly wasn't beyond the realm of possibility that we were Irish. We really *wanted* to be Irish. Who doesn't love lep-rechauns? Like a lot of children, we wanted to find one as a pet. And don't redheads just look terrific in green?

Don't get me wrong; we did have some culture from my father's side. We had a paternal grandmother, Muriel Laura Bolton (Gerry). Or Granny to us. She was a hoot, and we loved her to death. She was a crazy, brilliant, alcoholic, artist, nurse and grandmother – a total eccentric.

Sadly, she died when we were still children. God, I loved that woman. Still do. Doesn't most everyone really love their grand-parents? I miss her to this day. She was the first one to recognize and nurture my artistic ability. That counts for a lot. She helped turn on my soul. My mother never had that sort of experience with grandparents. I don't think she ever had grandparents, even adopted ones. If she did, she never spoke about them to us. Again, why was that?

Muriel was from Britain. And she was *very* British, with her tea and her accent and her interests. We loved getting yelled at by Granny because she would chastise us for "being cheeky." It was fun to listen to her get mad because it was always "bloody kids," "bloody this," and "bloody that." Our mother always got annoyed when we mimicked our grandmother and tried to incorporate her 'bloody' language into our lexicon. My mother wasn't having any of that and to this day none of us are 'bloody' women.

Yet my mother actually threw herself into the British culture. Who knows why? Maybe to be a good daughter-in-law? A good wife? Maybe it was a desperate attempt to adopt a heritage? Any heritage.

Here's an example of her urge toward a cultural connection; at Christmas and on our father's birthday, she made English trifle. Or – let me put it another way – she *tried* to make English trifle, remember her culinary skills. Trifle is supposed to be a British dessert made with fruit, home-made custard and a thin layer of home-made sponge cake soaked in sherry or fortified wine. It is then layered into a glass bowl to show off its beauty and bounty. It is, of course, the Anti-American Heart Association poster child for an unhealthy dessert.

My mother's version was no healthier than the real thing, but much, much … not British. She made it with Welches jelly, instant vanilla Jell-O pudding, lady fingers from the Grand Union, and whipped cream from the can. (Boy, I can still remember squirting that into my mouth.) Anyway, as much as we all loved it, I am sure it was a far cry from the real thing. To this day, I've never had real British trifle.

But the fact that she worked so hard to make a heritage for us and herself though was both sweet and sad.

What would it have been like if she had known about her own biological family origins? Would she have instead focused on Jameson, soda bread or Irish stew? Or Wiener schnitzel and streusel? Would her willingness to become a supportive 'British' wife have been so strong if she had her own cultural identity? She encouraged my father in his crazy British tea oddities, like agreeing to never washing his tea mug. That allowed the tea residue to build up for years on the inside of the mug. He insisted it made his tea taste better. She agreed that he could have one filthy cup of his own to do as he pleased. She promised to never wash it either. I am sure it killed her to do so as the inside of that tea mug was as black as night. To me it was totally disgusting. My father never had to worry about anyone using his special tea mug.

Our paternal grandfather left my grandmother and their children – my father and his brother – after the younger boy was born. He was not around for his own children or his grandchildren. I'm told that I met him once as an infant, and that he died shortly afterward. I wish that I had known him and that he was a part of my life. He was apparently a very bright man. I don't blame him for leaving my granny, but it would have been nice if he had been in my dad's life.

Although my father wasn't biologically or legally an orphan, he was also raised without a parent. That is certainly a theme in this family. I was told that my dad's father would come to take him to a ball game and buy him a suit once a year. That's odd right? He'd stay remotely involved with my father, but not really emotionally or physically present. It seems as close to abandonment as one can get without actually being abandoned. There is a plethora of research that validates how being separated from a parent can cause life long physical, behavioral and emotional health impacts. This was certainly a wound for my father. Was that a bond that my parents had with each other? Was not being raised by both biological parents a 'thing' for them?

For us, though, it was all about Granny. She was our only real grandparent, our only connection to the past – our past, our culture. We happily became British grand daughters with her, while simultaneously watching our other 'grandmother', Lucille Ball, on tv as much as we could. We could touch and breathe with our Granny. With Lucy we could admire her and feel the blessing of being connected to such an amazing grandmother through a small black and white box in our living room. Lucy was there every day; that counted. Our granny was nearby but we didn't see her daily. Lucy was also beautiful and so very funny. It was fun to brag to our friends that Lucy was our grandmother. I have to admit though, we did wonder why Lucy never came to visit us? Or even meet us? What was up with that? For a while in our childhoods, we joined a gazillion fan clubs of TV shows. Lucy's was certainly one of them.

And although my sisters and I weren't orphans, our parents combined had only one living biological and/or adoptive parent between them. That lack of connection to most of our ancestors, to our culture and family history seeped into the muck of our own sense of selves. Sometimes it was hard to understand the impact of it all. I episodically would try to sort it out and just wound up being even more confused. It was sort of like waking up from a dream. Where for an instant you can remember the names, faces and stories of the dream, but they fade into oblivion in a nano second. It was like trying to grasp and keep a firefly lit in your hands on a summer night. Fleeting stuff. Barely noticeable. Yet somehow the most crucial thing to know. Life saving knowledge?

I didn't pay that much conscious attention to the adoption stuff.

Until I did.

My mother died never knowing where she came from, where her people were from. She never knew what I was to eventually find out. She would never find the answers to her mysteries. She tried so hard to find out who she was but in the end didn't get any answers. She never knew that really *was* about three quarters Irish, as it turns out. And about a quarter German, too. Even as I write this, it still stuns me that I now know this. I know this unknowable thing. Living with a secret for so many decades, seems to somehow breathe life into the secret? Making it almost become alive. Real. The secret becomes a bit like a family member.

Always there. Always lurking just below the surface ready to rise up.

5

THE HEART HOLE GROWS BEYOND THE ORPHANS

I THINK IT'S HARD FOR people who know their family – where their people are from, the family food and cultural rituals, the family stories and the family history – to really imagine what it's like to not feel moored to people, stories, times, pictures.

Humans, in the deepest part of our hearts, are social beings. That has always been true, even going back to the time of cave people. We need to feel connected, to *be* connected. It's in our biological make-up. We need to know what's floating through our DNA. I did not really understand that until I started this quest.

Before I go further, I want to be clear that I think adoption is a beautiful and amazing thing. At one point, I had even considered adopting foster kids myself. This book is not meant to minimize the importance of adoption at all, or the sense of family and be-longing that an adopted family can offer a child. I am in awe of the sacred act of adopting and loving a child. I'm simply honoring the curiosity that most kids have about their own bloodlines. That's not a reflection on the adoptive family or the adoption process. I believe that adoption curiosity just is what every thinking, wondering person must go through as part of becoming their own person.

I will also frequently use the word "illegitimate" when I describe my mother's situation. I absolutely believe that no child should ever be considered illegitimate or is illegitimate! I use that term in this book more as an homage to the historical beliefs and attitudes of the day. The times in which these events occurred. I believe it is how my mother would have described her situation. The times have changed for the better, and erasing the stigma of being "illegitimate" is a wonderful gift to any child.

When I started having my own kids, my mother was already dead. The birth of my first son Max awakened something in me. I wanted my own children to know where they came from, who their people were. Heck, *I* wanted to know who I was. I thought it was simple curiosity but, if I am honest, it was becoming important to me and important to my heart.

I remember how my son Max was after he was born. I had been carrying twins but lost one before I even knew there was a second baby. When I began to bleed, a colleague drove me to the hospital where I was told I was losing one of the babies. I became so focused on making sure the baby I still carried was safe and not in danger that I didn't really process the loss of the second one. I barely even thought about it then. Today, my reaction seems so odd to me, but back then it didn't.

Interestingly, as a toddler Max would often lay on top of the cats, pillows, toys or something else and ask, "Could someone please lie on top of me?" My husband and I had to put something heavy

on top of him, and he would entwine himself in it. He would try
to spoon with the cats and was constantly in a knot with pillows,
blankets and toys. It finally occurred to me that this behavior
might have been a "missing my twin thing." Could that be true?
Can we really still remember in utero connections after birth? In
our non verbal brain places? Is the primal connection really that
deep? Forever? It is mind boggling to me.

That's when the magnitude of losing the other baby hit me.

Perhaps not knowing your family might be like missing your unknown twin? Knowing something isn't quite right, something's
missing, but not being able to put a finger on it? Maybe. I don't
really know. To this day, Max still wraps himself around pillows
when he sleeps. He's a grown man. Does the loss run that deep
for eternity?

When I began to be deeply curious about my mother's adoption
and the child she had given up, I contacted Donald, my mother's
adopted brother. My uncle sent me a pile of letters that he had
exchanged with their cousin Elsie, Jennie Gray's niece, about his
and my mother's adoption.

When I read those letters, I felt a wave of sadness for them both.

Donald had always reminded me of Bing Crosby. He kind of
looked like Bing and smoked a pipe. He was a sweet and playful
man. His yearning to know his own story was so powerful that
even as a successful, seemingly happy man in his 60s, his desperation to find the truth about his biological family seemed as
intense as a lost child in the dark trying to find the light switch.
Things swirl around in the dark sometimes. I was pretty shocked
and honored that he shared the letters – and his own vulnerabil-
ity – with me.

In a letter to me, my uncle wrote, "As for your mother, I believe that she always, in her mind, resented the fact that she was an unwanted child by her biological birth mother. It is too bad that Barbara had that fixation because the mother that we knew loved us equally."

Feeling unwanted – what a horrifying burden for a child. A fixation?

Why was it presented like that? Instead of reframed as the biological family giving the Grays a precious gift?

For me, reading that part of my uncle's letter was like a balloon getting popped, then blasting through the room willy-nilly until the air is gone. Then it abruptly just stops moving, and lies on the floor like a dead thing. My heart broke into a thousand tears for that poor child. My poor mother. That is soul-breaking stuff.

My uncle's words naturally triggered the memory of my mother's desperate attempt to get some clues out of old Aunt Nellie about her own adoption. The memory blasted through me like the heat of a shot of whiskey going down my throat. Only there's no high afterward. Just isolation and a bit of desperation.

Knowing that people I loved so much had such huge, black heart holes left me with overwhelming feelings of impotence and sadness. Sadness that I couldn't fix this for them. Or fix me.

The glimmer that this heart hole was in me, too, was just starting to really flicker. The lighting bug thing again. The light is suddenly on, then abruptly goes off. Easy to forget. Easy to lose

I had made a few phone calls and wrote a few letters trying to get records and information, but they were all dead ends. I had planned to look into it further. I was absolutely going to find my sibling and grandparents!

But babies, toddlers, diapers and work eclipsed all else for a long, long time.

I wouldn't really get back to it full throttle for a couple of decades.

6

DAWN AND THE DNA TEST

IT WAS MY SISTER DAWN who got me back on track.

On a lark, Dawn decided to take a DNA test. She says her motivation was to find to what her ethnicity was. See? There it is again. Most people don't wonder that. They just know what their ethnicity is, or at least think they do. I would find out in the research for this book that almost everyone is surprised at some part of their DNA test results, their ethnicity or who they wind up being related to.

I was mildly interested in what was discovered. My hope was that we would find out that we had some Native American blood in us. I've always felt connected to that culture and would have been thrilled to find some link to those magnificent, beautiful spiritual people. Is this my Native American version of my mother's immersion into being a good British wife? Do regular people do this too? Regular people who know who they are.

But in reality, I wasn't all that interested in Dawn's DNA test. I was no more than mildly curious.

Her results came back in March of 2012. A bit of Irish luck?

Her DNA showed that she was about 50 percent Irish, 24 percent Western European, 18 percent British and Welsh, and 7 percent Scandinavian. The remaining 1 percent was registered as low confidence.

Despite our childhood speculation about red hair and freckles, my sisters and I were shocked to learn that indeed we really are mostly Irish. We never had a real concrete clue. Our mother lived her life and died never knowing that she was likely almost completely Irish. For her, a lifetime search for a cultural identity was a fruitless effort. My sister spits into a test tube and finds out in six weeks. Life can be so odd.

To be honest, I had never even heard of European countries being grouped as Western European. I was kind of embarrassed that I had to look it up. The countries of Western Europe include Belgium, the Netherlands, Switzerland, Luxembourg, France, Germany and Liechtenstein. Liechtenstein? I had never even heard of that country before the test results came in. I know all about it now, though.

It would turn out later that these results would prove to be right on target.

I was initially stunned at the Scandinavian results. But after thinking about it and recalling the Viking raping and pillaging stuff, I realized that nearly everyone – particularly the Irish, Scots and Brits – probably has a bit Scandinavian blood. It is said that the native Irish and the Vikings eventually co-mingled and wound up blending their cultures and, surprisingly, became one community. My sisters are tall like Vikings. Dawn is about 6' and Billie is over 5'8". At 5'6", I'm the runt of the family. I call them Vikings.

After some processing, I found myself happy and content with the Scandinavian and Western European energy pumping through my blood.

What we were most surprised about, though, was that Dawn wasn't 50 percent British. How could that be? We presumed that as Granny was 100 percent British and that our paternal grandfather was also 100 percent British. See? There is is again. We just fill in the blanks about what we think might be true and then believe it to be true. Why would we presume that our paternal grandfather was also 100 percent British? Again, was it part of a primal search for a culture? Obviously, Granny wasn't as English as she thought she was. Otherwise, Dawn's DNA would have come up at least 25 percent English.

I didn't realize then that DNA isn't really like a math formula though. There's tremendous variation in what gets passed down, even from one sibling to the next.

Thinking about it now, I realize how my father's abandonment by his father must have had an impact on, not only him, but also on my sisters and me. Who was he anyway? Who were we? I have to admit that the genealogical results were initially a little disconcerting but, in that way our family has, we just sort of moved on and didn't really think much more about it. Denial is such a wonderful gift sometimes.

Besides, I was thinking about other things. Not Dawn's DNA.

In 2012, Max was twenty years old and living in Oakland,

California, with a friend. He was going through his young adult "gotta get away from home, no matter what the cost" stage. It was during the height of the Occupy Movement, the progressive political uprising against social and economic inequality. My son was just blocks from the epicenter.

One night during the height of a demonstration, he agreed to use a cardboard shield and walk toward the police, who were trying to control the crowd. I didn't realize how close he was to it all until I saw a video of him running from the police, who were shooting rubber bullets at the demonstrators. He wound up getting arrested for a night.

Worse, he watched a man in his holding cell nearly die of a ruptured spleen as a result of being beaten by the police.

My other son, Zack, was eighteen years old, just graduating from high school and heading to a Catholic college in Massachusetts that was a total mismatch for him. He chose that school because his two best friends were going there. Bad decision academically. Great decision for the friendships.

Any parent reading this can understand how worry and powerlessness over our children's lives can be a bit of a distraction. No one tells you when you have a child, that the dormant 'Worry' gene kicks on the second you hold your baby.

It's funny how my quest to find my family seemed to episodically fade in and out of my thoughts.

I didn't think much about my sister's DNA results. In fact, I forgot about it. Until my own life changed.

7

LOUIS THE ITALIAN AND HIS ATTACHMENT TO FAMILY

FAST FORWARD TO 2016.

Four years after the Dawn's DNA results came in.

I wound up divorced from a man whom I thought was the love of my life. Like most divorces, it was painful and all encompassing. I certainly wasn't focused on my sister's DNA. It was the very last thing I was thinking of.

My thoughts were on my children and my stepchildren. How was I going to start this new life I found myself in?

But I did okay. I found out that I was stronger than I realized, and I picked myself up.

A couple of years after my ex-husband and I split up, I started dating Louis. Boy, was he a different sort of man. At the time, he was an active duty firefighter with the Fire Department of New York City. That was a big plus for me. After the World Trade Center towers and buildings came down in New York City, when this country was attacked on September 11, 2001, I worked for the FDNY myself for about 5 years. I learned how good most of these men were.

When I first met Louis, I was initially underwhelmed. He seemed shy, quiet, even a little awkward. Maybe a little unexciting? Shamefully I thought that he'd be too much work to bother with.

Was I full of myself or what? Again, I wasn't going to include these thoughts in the book, but I need to tell my truths also. I embarrass myself.

Anyway, we went out to lunch on our first date in Greenwood Lake, in Orange County, New York, where I had grown up and where he had spent summers with his family as a child. Both of us were surprised that we had never met before. It isn't a big town and everyone knows everyone.

I think our mutual history and curiosity spurred the date on. During lunch we realized that we knew many of the same people and places. My granny had been the nurse for the woman who owned the bungalows where his family had stayed in the summer. Supposedly, the two of them were great drinking buddies. Did he remember a short, stout, British woman who was possibly tipsy and driving a rickety old blue pickup truck?

It turned out that Louis and I had probably even seen each other at *Ground Zero,* the site of the World Trade Towers collapse, as we were there at the same times. We discovered that we had taken our kids skiing at the same places, that we had worked in the same building in New York City while working for the Fire

Department, and we both had gone apple picking with our kids at the same place. It's like we were in parallel universes swirling around each other for a lifetime, like the Milky Way. How did I not know of him? He was friends with one of my best childhood friend's brothers.

We really were from two different universes, though.

Even on our first date, Louis talked about his family. The ancestors. He told me about how and why his grandparents and uncles and aunts came to America from Sicily and Genoa, Italy, and how they had landed on the Lower East Side of New York City. To this day, he has children, nephews and cousins living within blocks of where the elders had lived. He describes himself as having grown up under the shadow of the iconic Brooklyn Bridge. That bridge remains a touchstone for his life until this day.

He detailed the part of Italy where his people had come from, why they left and what they did when they arrived in New York City. I was sort of stunned listening to someone talk with such reverence about parents, grandparents and the old homeland. He talked about all that his immigrant relatives sacrificed and endured to get to this Promised Land. Of how hard it must have been to leave everyone and everything they knew to travel to a dark, cold city where they did not speak the language. To go where everything was so foreign to them – the climate, the culture, the language, the food, the metropolitan views. He was so eloquent when he spoke of how tenacious they had been to endure so much change, chaos and trauma. Yet they had survived and thrived.

That was all on our first date.

What the heck was that all about?

I couldn't tell if he was from an alien spaceship or if I was? Was this all legit, I wondered. Who the heck pulls out the honoring the ancestors play on a first date? Was he the geek, or was I the superficial and shallow one because I had never really thought about these things? Is this what people with relatives think like? Was my shock another symptom of being raised by an orphan? There is no way my mother could have taught me these things. I remember going to France years ago and having such struggles communicating and understanding everything. I had become so overwhelmed with how new and unusual all of the food tasted to me while I was in Paris, that I finally just ordered a piece of toast. Something simple and familiar. I nearly cried when they brought it out with a scoop of moldy cheese melting all over it. It's hard to process so many new things at once like that. It was befuddling for me to be in such a foreign place. I kind of felt that same way on my first date with Louis.

I felt a bit unnerved. Is this what regular people talk about? Is this how people with family histories and stories think? I was beginning to wonder if perhaps I had missed a huge part of my emotional and familial development.

I was expecting the sex move, not the honoring the ancestors move.

I was beginning to understand that I too, really did have a big hole in my heart, that there really was something missing and something really wrong. Something big. Something crucial. I think before I was suspecting it and sort of, kind of, realizing that something was not quite right. I had the intuition and the suspicion, but I don't think I really allowed myself to totally acknowledge and accept that something had happened to me and my own heart.

I unknowingly caught the same condition that my mother had! Good grief. To be honest, the epiphany was a bit unnerving for me. It's like those dreams when all of your teeth fall out because you forgot to tie them into your mouth. Weird but true. And yet it was oddly soothing to be able to finally name it.

Louis is a historian and has a degree in history. He has a way of seeing things from the long road. I, too, consider myself a bit of a history buff. I am really into Native American history, Revolutionary War history, history of the Samurai. It never really entered my mind in a conscious way to wonder much about my own history.

How could that even be? My little world was really rocked.

Thank God!

Listening to Louis made me realize that my sisters and I all wound up with men from big families. Families...Something we didn't really have. Was it a coincidence? How could it be that all of our men had four siblings and a strong ethnic and cultural identity? Interestingly, they all hooked up with women with no real ethnic identity. We three sisters wound up easily merging into strong families. Happily merging into big families.

Dawn's husband Joe is Polish. Think polka, pierogies, stuffed cabbage and sauerkraut. I remember being stunned at Dawn's bridal shower where the future sisters-in-law had made dishes with three different types of cabbage: stuffed cabbage, sauerkraut and coleslaw. What other family would that happen in? It seemed pretty cool to have such a strong cultural identity.

I remember Joe's ninety-something-year-old mother trying to teach me how to polka. I was totally shamed by her because of my lack of rhythm. Ha! To this day I feel bad that I never really learned to polka. She was always encouraging about my polka disability, sort of the way one is while watching a slow-witted child learn to tie shoes.

My other brother-in-law, Dave, and his siblings went to his mother's home every Sunday for dinner. Cousins, aunts, uncles, siblings, all getting together for a Sunday meal. Keeping the family together. It's like a Norman Rockwell painting, right?

How could this be? How could three women without much of an ethnic family background or even family, wind up with men with such strong family ties and with so much emphasis on family tradition?

Well, how could we not?

Anyway. Louis is a man of Italian descent. His grandparents came to America from Italy. For him, it's all about family. Who talks about their parents and grandparents on a first date? Hearing about his strong bond to his family was like doing crack (not that I ever actually *did* crack), it was addictive. He was connected to them all, both dead and alive. He was awakening in me a new way to think about myself. About my family. I never knew that I didn't know how to think and absorb it all.

I casually mentioned my sister's DNA test showing that I was mostly Irish. I think I just tossed that in as it was pretty much all I had to contribute to the conversation about ancestors. A little genealogical mini-grenade. Who wouldn't be bowled over by that? Ha! Remember we were on a first date and I was trying to be impressive.

Well, Louis exploded with ten million questions that I never thought about let alone talked about. But sadly there was not a single question I could answer. I wound up telling him about the baby give-away, orphan mother story. I think that was the only time I've ever seen him totally silent? Just for a nano-second, though. Then there were a thousand more questions.

Was this really his prelude to the sex move? What the heck was happening? What kind of date was this?

He was certainly careening past my initial assessment of him as a little boring and shy. Remember, this was our first date. It was a very new approach to a relationship for me. I didn't realize then how much he was going to change my life forever. What a gift he's been. How did I get to be so lucky? Maybe the Irish luck was pouring down on my little heart hole? His 'Cup of Kindness' never seemed to empty.

Robin with Louis Trazino, who became both guide and cheerleader in her search for her family.

A couple of dates later, we were at home where there was a computer. Like a pick pocket accidentally bumping into his next victim, Louis casually said, "Oh, hey, let's check out your sister's DNA test." That sounds simple and reasonable right? Sort of unmalignant. Casual even.

But what happened next changed my life forever.

He understood how to read the DNA levels and their significance in potential family relationships. He also saw that a second cousin had written to my sister a year or so prior happily asking to figure out how they were connected. Naturally, my sister had no clue about any sort of connection and sort of inadvertently shut them down. How could my sister possibly know who was or wasn't connected to us? How could she know what the family names were? How could she know where our people were from?

The cousin was Italian and Irish. As Dawn had no Italian in her, they both assumed they were related through the Irish line. The cousin graciously told Dawn that one of their Irish grandparents was a Kelly. We figured out later that the cousin was actually a first half cousin! Wow.

Ancestry shows all of the 1st – 4th cousins. I had cousins! When one opens the site they are just all right there. Wow. I saw that I had a couple of hundred cousins now. Holy cow! I immediately loved them all. Not really – but it really was thrilling.

I was now in a genealogical spaceship happily careening toward the event horizon of my own dark heart hole.

8

MEETING THE COUSINS

So after absorbing Louis's love of family, family history and the thrill of a gosh darn good mystery, I found myself starting to get charged up about this quest again. He made me believe it might actually be possible to find my grandparents. His mantra for the next two years was, "The records are there. We just have to figure out where to look."

Could that really be true? Or had I inadvertently hooked up with a really crazy, odd man? I decided that if he was crazy, he seemed harmless. What could it hurt? I did come to understand that he was odd, but a sweet odd. And he was an amazing, tireless, encouraging genealogical partner. I absolutely couldn't have done it without him.

He taught me how to understand the cousin line-up on Ancestry.com, the DNA service Dawn had chosen. I also then tested with Ancestry.com and MyHeritage. The first people in the list were the closest relatives. We focused on first to third cousins. It was still blowing me away to learn that Dawn, Billie and I now had hundreds of cousins. I was used to having only four. I think the enormity of that last sentence is easy to overlook, but think about it. We went from having four cousins who we saw once or twice a year during our childhood to having hundreds of cousins all over the world. We were part of a clan. A family!

I was starting to feel a little less orphany.

I was completely new to this sort of thing, and at first I wound up blasting my way through cousins like those sharks that tear apart the bloody chum in a feeding frenzy. I feel very embarrassed now by my ignorance and tendency to go too fast and tell people too much too soon. I expected that people would immediately know who I was and would just tell me my place in the family. I didn't understand at first that I had to figure it out myself. No one was keeping a secret about an orphan.

And I didn't realize that not everyone would necessarily want to hear theories about illegitimate secret babies or illegal baby giveaways that their beloved relatives may have had. Go figure. Most didn't mind though, and in fact many more were unbelievably encouraging and helpful. Their cup of kindness and compassion is why I now respond to everyone who contacts me. Paying it back.

Anyway, one of the first cousins I contacted was Pattie from Oregon. It turns out that she was a professional genealogist, one of her many skills. She's quite the Renaissance woman. She has even taught courses on genealogy, and she's paid to find lost relatives for people. Lucky me, right? I never hit it big with lottery tickets, but I frequently hit the jackpot with cousins.

Anyway, it was while I was literally poking around in her profile that I discovered the "Shared Matches" tab on Ancestry.com. I clicked on it and immediately realized that all of the people that

Pattie and I both matched with had a Dooley in their family. Of course, I immediately concluded that I, too, was a Dooley. It didn't dawn on me for months that they were all part of Pattie's family, not mine, and that she managed them all. It seems so stupid to me now, but then it made perfect sense in a befuddled sort of way.

It gets worse.

I decided that I should put her relatives on my tree in case anyone was out there looking for me. That way, I could see who shows up. Good God! Who does that? Was I that desperate? Yup.

When I told Pattie my plan, she didn't tell me to pull myself together or go find my own family. She just let me sort of "borrow" her family for a bit until I got my brain working better. We went through all of the branches of her tree trying to rule everyone in or out. She had Kellys in her family, too, but there didn't seem to be a connection. I later found out that Kelly is the second most common Irish name, just behind Murphy. There's a billion gazillion Kelly's. And some of them were related to me!

I learned so much from her about how to do a methodical search though. I was starting to get beyond genealogical kindergarten.

As we worked together, we wound up becoming very fond of each other. One day, she spontaneously said, "You need to come out to Oregon to see me." I just as spontaneously said, "Sure! I will. Thanks." I hung up the phone and bought a ticket.

I got off the phone and told my two adult sons, Max and Zack, that I was going to Oregon to see my new cousin.

Silence...

Then … "Are you nuts? You don't even know her! What if she kills you? This is totally weird and creepy. Please don't go." Okay, I need to put this in context. We're from New York. Everyone thinks like that in New York. Still, they did have kind of a point.

Interestingly, though, they had a friend who then invited them to go to some sort of hippie festival in Eugene, Oregon. Next thing I know, we were all going to Oregon.

As this journey progressed, I found that there were many, many coincidences like that. It made me feel that Karma? The finger of God? Fate?, was at work here. I honestly feel I had angels walking with me. For real.

Around that same time, I contacted another cousin, Mary Ellen. Lightning struck twice. She was besties with a genealogist. Another one who gave courses on genealogy! How crazy is that? There's the finger of God again. I was a walking God fingerprint.

Mary Ellen was a relatively high DNA cousin. But better than that, she really, really wanted to figure out the mystery of how we were connected. Sooo … her genealogist buddy wound up doing my father's complete family tree on both of his parents, looking to see if that's where my match was with Mary Ellen. I was stunned. I just couldn't believe it. It would have taken me a thousand years to do that then. And it was just done for me. Wow. I wound up feeling very close and connected to them too.

They were in Washington state, and I made plans to see them, while on the West coast. It was going to be a cousin holiday! I had maternal cousins! It's still so difficult to describe what it meant to me to be meeting folks connected to my mother's family. She never knew she had a family, yet here I was going to meet them. There was a surreal quality to the whole thing, sort of like watching your life with 3D glasses on. Who's the orphan daughter now? Not me. I was going to meet maternal relatives.

My sons loved Pattie and her husband, Don. Me too. Pattie took us through the high desert of Oregon and taught us desert things. I had no clue Oregon even had deserts. I thought it was just filled with snow-covered mountains. Who knew?

She even took us and with her grandkids to a secret, sacred cave with Native American petroglyphs. Pattie does land management surveys and reports and winds up learning forgotten things and places. The cave was literally in the ground and we had to hike to it and then climb down into it. It was almost like a mouth in the world.

The cave was thrilling for me. In my twenties, I had taught myself to "read" and interpret rock paintings and petroglyphs. Before I had children, I had taken a solitary vacation to the sites in the southwest while the desert was in bloom to read the rocks and see the desert flowers. What a gift she gave us. Pattie showed us where the flint knappers had worked and left their shiny, black, obsidian flakes during ancient Native American gatherings. The chards were even still there in little piles next to sitting rocks. Holy cow! I was literally on sacred pathways in every sense of the word. Sadly, the Native Americans were not my ancestors (at least not in this life), but there was certainly an ancestor energy and reverence for the ancient ones in the air. My sons wound up going deep within the cave; there was even ice far below. We were there in July. What a metaphor for my family quest. The ice was thawing.

There was such a primal quality to the whole experience for me. I was literally in a sacred place in time and space, sort of an Einsteinium experience. Everything was bending in my brain.

It was almost as if ancient ancestor energy was starting to work into me. These ancient Native Americans has left messages for their ancestors thousands of years ago. Here I was with one of my new Irish relatives. Was their ancestor energy working into my DNA? Awakening something in me? Something almost primal? God, I sure hoped so.

Pattie and I worked on some ancestry stuff and she taught me about more genealogical and historical resources. Ultimately, we didn't discover anything new and precise about our grandparents or exactly how we were connected to each other. I later learned that our 3rd great grandmothers were from the same little town, Ahascragh, Ireland. We didn't know that then though. It was such a tiny town with such a small gene pool, that somewhere some Kelly likely hooked up with a Dooley (or maybe one of her Donnellans). We never figured out exactly which one though.

It was very sad to say goodbye to Pattie and Don as we all felt connected forever now. We would see them again, a year later, when they traveled to New York to stay with us and discovered a new answer to a genealogical hole in her family.

Max and Zack met their friend and went to the hippie festival while I headed up to Washington. Now I am a hot stinking mess with technology. I had made plans to meet Mary Ellen around ten a.m., but I had forgotten to adjust my watch to account for the time difference. I showed up way early. Mary Ellen still had her pj's on. I didn't want to embarrass her more than she already was for not being ready for my visit, so I left to get a cup of coffee while she pulled herself together. Washington and Oregon were amazing places to find really good coffee. I was thinking that maybe this new cousin was kind of slow? Or maybe socially confused? Good grief! It took me a while to realize that it was all me. It was *my* mistake. *I* was the slow one. We still laugh about that.

She had made me a folder of her last trip to Ireland and a list of her relatives. That was such a sweet and kind thing to do. We would later learn that she was also related to Pattie. Her people were from the same small town in County Galway, Ireland, Ahascragh, but again we didn't know that then. My heart was touched forever. We never did figure out our connection to each other during that trip. Her people were Leonards. There were several Leonards who married Kellys in that part of Ireland. Probably a Dooley married a Leonard too.

But I did get a treasure or two from them. Mary Ellen's genealogist friend told me about the Bettinger DNA chart. It's online and it's free. (If you decide to use it, be sure to get the latest version.) Basically, it delineates the likely DNA Centimorgan range one could expect for each relationship (siblings, half siblings, first cousins, kids, aunts, half aunts, and so on).

Centimorgans are the amount of shared genetic material in our DNA. The higher the number, the closer the relationship. It became one of the most valuable tools in my search. I was surprised, though, to learn that there's a big DNA range. For example, the centimorgan count for a half sibling could be 1,317–2,312, with the average being about 1,783. That's about a 1,000 centimorgan differential for the same relationship. This stuff is hard, really hard.

I've also learned that DNA is pretty fickle. For example, Dawn has a centimorgan count of about 45 with Pattie. I barely show up as anything with Pattie. The Bettinger chart puts that level at about a half third cousin once removed. Ancestry puts it as fourth cousin. Dawn and I each turned up cousins that the other didn't, and we are full sisters. Weird and confusing.

The other gem Mary Ellen's friend taught me is that on Ancestry. com, there is a little circle with a little "I" in it next to the

Confidence Bar when opening up a relative's profile. That shows the centimorgan count. I now consider myself the centimorgan princess. Ancestry finally just started displaying the centimorgan count directly. What a welcome revision!

After leaving Mary Ellen, I went to Oregon to get my sons. We decided to go back to Washington to see the HOH temperate rainforest. I had never even heard of that before. It was utterly magnificent. It is classified as a World Heritage Site, and rightly so. All of us were struck with wonder and awe. Turns out that's where the *Twilight* movies were filmed – in Fork, Washington. The whole town is now vampire themed.

The trees there are so old and so massive that I found myself wondering about the world history that the trees silently had lived through. As I had just come from meeting these two new Irish cousins, How could I not think about the history that these trees had 'witnessed'? These ancestor experiences put me in the place where I was realizing how time passes and we all fade; yet the world keeps turning. Trees grow older and bigger, families get flung to new continents and start new families. And those families then lose track of their own time and their own history.

Soon after returning home, my sister Dawn and I met a couple other Dooley DNA cousins – Tom and Sharon Dooley – in upstate New York. Again, I found that we were related to sweet, decent, good humans. They were not aware of any connection to Pattie, but we were clearly related to the Dooley clan.

Tom had two Dooley aunts and a Dooley mom (all sisters) whom they referred to as The Flory Dory Girls. The Flory Dory girls are all dead now, but they were all very beautiful and very sociable. One of them was even a lingerie model. That's close to being an actress, right? Would a lingerie model be more likely to get pregnant and have to give the baby up? Well, why not? I was certain that she was a likely candidate for a grandmother. I was getting better at this! By now, I was in genealogical third grade.

But alas, it didn't take me long to realize that I wasn't a Flory Dory granddaughter. Any of the Flory Dory girls would have produced a very high centimorgan count with us and Tom Dooley as they were alive at the same time that we were. They wouldn't have been so far removed genealogically. I was slowly learning to really understand the centirmorgan counts and their significance. I never would have made an assumption like that today, but back then it was a Flory Dory possibility

It was clear that this quest was going to be harder and far more complex than I had ever anticipated. I wasn't sure what to do next.

Louis was always terrific when I hit a wall. He always had one more thought or one more suggestion. But even he couldn't have predicted what would come next.

No one could.

9

FINDING JOE KELLY

THIS IS THE PART OF the book that gets a little technical, and the chapter I most worried about writing. I don't presume to be any sort of expert with the science behind DNA. But I have bumbled my way through and picked up some basic understanding of how it all works. It's one of the most important things to understand for anyone who wants to undertake an ancestor search. For me, this is what changed everything – changed my life forever!

I undertook this quest to find my grandparents, but I knew pretty much nothing about this sort of research, DNA, genealogy or adoption. Heck, I didn't even know how to understand family history in general, much less my own. I didn't have one credible clue.

Except my DNA …

Louis became my informal mentor on how and what to research. The paper trail. He had done some spectacular work years before on piecing his own family story together. To do a search one needs to use both records and DNA. For starters, he took me to the New York City Hall of Archives. From the first moment I found a bit of information I was looking for, I was addicted. What a thrill! My serotonin receptors were firing like those firecrackers that scramble on the ground like little animals.

Louis was just as excited. We were geeks in love. My son Zack complained one night as we were excitedly going over our findings and planning the next research target, that, "You two are too boring and just too much. You're laughing too much and you're way too loud."

To this day, that remains one of the best compliments I ever got. We've laughed about that a thousand times.

Among the things that I didn't even know at the outset of this quest was the definition of second cousins (grandparents were siblings), third cousins (great-grandparents were siblings), first cousins once removed (the children of first cousins) and so on. Why would I know this? There was no need. I had just two first cousins from my Uncle Donald and two from my father's brother. That was it. Not much.

I learned the importance of doing DNA testing with more than one site. Each site interprets the results slightly differently, but more than that, each company has different people registered. Different relatives. Louis says it's like putting a fishing pole in many ponds. I began with Ancestry and My Heritage. Louis suggested I then upload my DNA results onto GEDmatch, a free DNA site with a worldwide platform. Through GEDmatch, I was able to find even more cousins in Ireland and England. To be honest, though, that site was a little too technical for me, but the more sites you're on, the better you are, genealogically speaking.

We actually found an article on line that gave the GEDmatch numbers for prehistoric bones. Get this, Louis and I found our that we were from the same tribe about 7500 years ago. We were actually related to two different skeletons. He says it took us 7500 years to find each other. This stuff can be really fun.

There's a lot of conversations now about law enforcement using GEDmatch to catch murderers and rapists. I honestly don't care because I am not a felon on the run. I am not trying to cover up a murder or any other sort of crime. No one is looking for my DNA. I personally had nothing to lose and everything to gain. I honestly feel happy that these psychopaths are getting caught and imprisoned after decades of getting away with murder.

One of my favorite genealogy sites is Family Search, sponsored by the Church of the Latter Day Saints (Mormons). They don't require DNA. Genealogical research is an important part of their religion because they believe the eternal joining of families is possible. It is therefore important to them then, to know who our ancestors are. They have dedicated themselves to archiving worldwide genealogy records and making them FREE to anyone who wants them. This is a really good place to start if you already know who your parents and grandparents are. Their site likely has more information on your family than you do. They collaborate with the DNA companies and have access to their data too. A few times I found that Family Search had information that the others didn't. They are happy to offer free help and support to anyone trying to figure out their family history. The sister missionaries who I worked with were always happy to help me learn their system and graciously tolerated my technological struggles. More than that, they were enthusiastic and encouraging partners. They too advised me not to give up and keep trying despite how little I had to start with.

The most valuable lesson I learned through these various sites is that the more places we test and the more tests we take, the more likely we are to find a clue.

I learned why from Louis, who told me that siblings pick up different DNA from their parents. If they didn't, all siblings would be identical twins. And the more DNA samples out there, the more opportunities there are to find relatives. That explained why my sister always matches up with twenty to thirty more cousins that I do. As it turns out, I have more Irish DNA than she does.

It was crazy to me. I had so much to learn. Remember how hard the third-grade school year was? The tortuous year when we had to memorize the times tables? Remember how daunting that was? That's how I felt. I was completely overwhelmed.

The first cousin who had contacted my sister a couple of years before I jumped into this, told Dawn that a grandparent was named Kelly. We also got the last name of that Kelly's spouse. That cousin had very high centimorgan counts that matched us. Remember that centimorgans are the shared amount of genetic material. The higher the count, the closer the relative is. Ancestry estimated that this was a second cousin to us. That's close! Crazy close. But the Kelly name was unfamiliar to us. But all names would be unfamiliar to us, though, wouldn't they?

That was when Louis suggested that I upload DNA with Family Tree, another genealogy/DNA site. I did it. It was free. When those results came back, I found another cousin. This one was also a Kelly whose centimorgan count was even higher than that of our first cousin contact. It was in the first or second cousin range. And both cousins shared the same grandfather.

Joe Kelly.

I began to suspect that Joe Kelly might have been my grandfather, too, as no other cousins shared so much genetic material with me. That was a totally insane thought to me. Maybe I had a biological grandfather? My mother had a father and maybe I knew his name? I felt like a big snowflake blowing in a blizzard, never quite landing anywhere yet still blasting through a storm.

I tried to do a family tree for the first cousin who had contacted Dawn. I had the two last names; that was enough to get started. I wanted to find Joe Kelly. I found him all right – in New Jersey – but, unbeknownst to me, I found the wrong Joe Kelly. I found my grandfather's cousin, Joe Kelly. Yes, yes, yes, I learned that Irish families tend to recycle the same names. Who knew? Happily, I would discover that these two branches of the Kelly family were related to each other – and to me. Irish luck. Or maybe beginners luck?

For a while, though, I was convinced that the New Jersey Joe Kelly was *my* Joe Kelly. My grandfather. This is the learning curve stuff of genealogy. I'd never make that mistake today, but I sure jumped off the cliff like a dog chasing a squirrel then.

I contacted another cousin from the New Jersey Joe Kelly's family – Lorraine. On most of the genetic testing sites, you can email relatives. They may or may not email back, but most do. Lorraine, as it turned out, is a terrific evidence-based genealogist with an amazing tree. She is probably one of the best, most thorough genealogists I've met on this journey.

Lorraine was hesitant to believe that our grandparents were siblings. True, our centimorgan count was high-ish (about 45), but maybe not high enough. Nonetheless, she was gracious and willing to share information and pictures. She taught me so much. One of my theories at the time was that either Lorraine's grandmother's brother or sister was probably my grandparent. She seemed a little shocked and disbelieving, yet willing to consider the possibility.

I am kind of horrified about my genealogical ignorance then. I now understand how to approach people in a gentler way. I was like a puppy in a box. My only consolation is that, in my search for proof of my mother's birth, I found a previously unknown baby of one of Lorraine's beloved aunts. That's something I guess. I could pay her back a little bit for being so encouraging and giving a cup of kindness to her newest, most annoying cousin.

Lorraine's tree was magnificent. She had taken years to carefully research and corroborate her records. She had posted pictures, documents and best for me, a neon arrow to the exact town in Ireland that my Kelly family came from, Menlough, Ireland.

I actually now knew where in Ireland my mother's family started. For me it was like getting hit by a fireball. Happily getting hit by a fireball.

I decided I needed to go to Ireland and headed there believing that the wrong Joe Kelly was my grandfather.

10

GOING 'HOME' TO A PLACE I'VE NEVER BEEN

In September of 2017, my stepdaughter Lauren was studying abroad in Dublin. I love her and missed her, so what else could I do but use her as an excuse to go Ireland? It's what any decent step-mom would do, right?

Plus, there really were $99 flights to Ireland. A car rental in Ireland is less than $10 a day. How could I not go? I was in.

I had no real plan other than to try to find the Menlough/Vermount area of County Galway and drive around looking for the cottage and farm where James Kelly and his wife Nancy Carroll had lived and raised their kids. From Lorraine's tree, I'd learned that James was the earliest known Kelly, born about 1780. He was married to Nancy Carroll from Ahascragh, which is just a few miles from Menlough. Remember Ahascragh? The same town where my cousin Pattie's 3rd grandmother was from.

Lorraine had posted a picture of the cottage. I had it printed out and took it with me to Ireland. I realize that just driving around searching for a cottage really wasn't much of a plan, but was the best I could come up with.

James and Nancy were the great great-grandparents of both Joe Kellys. They had five sons: James, Hubert, Patrick, Michael and John Kelly. Were there really no girls? No one has been able to find any. I'm still not so sure about that though.

Although I wasn't aware of it, I had become totally confused about the two Joe Kelly cousins. Thankfully I didn't realize how befuddled I really was and was therefore totally unconcerned with it. The Joes were about the same age. One lived in Manhattan; the other lived across the Hudson River in Jersey City, New Jersey. They could have hung out together as they lived just a ferry ride away from one another. Their dads were cousins. Jersey Joe's father Patrick was Michael's son (mentioned above). Manhattan Joe's father Michael, was Patrick's son (mentioned above). That would confuse anyone, right?

Jersey Joe's father, Patrick, worked on the railroads in Jersey City. How? How would a young man who emigrated from County Galway, Ireland, as only a teenager even know about jobs in Jersey City? I learned later from an 'uncousin' on Ancestry, William Jennings, that there was an informal support system for families in County Galway to help and encourage Irish immigrants to head toward Jersey City, New Jersey. There was a 'Horseshoe District' in Jersey City. It was heavily Irish, and a good percentage of them worked in jobs connected to the railroad. The district was mapped out like the shape of a horseshoe with the railroads forming the U shape boundaries on three sides and the Hudson River forming the fourth side of the district.

William Jennings said his uncle, Dominick Jennings and Dominick's brothers were main players in this arrangement. In Ireland, the Jennings' lived within walking distance of the Menlough/Vermount region, where the Kellys were. I would suspect that the Kelly and the Jennings families had to have known of each other, as they were from such a small part of Ireland. Sort of like Middle Earth. The Jennings brothers had apparently worked with horses in Ireland. When they got to Jersey City, they were able to parlay that skill into driving truck horses and hauling coal to the trains. Dominick was among the emerging Irish leaders in Jersey City who had a part in forming a teamsters union. The union helped lift Irish workers out of poverty and give them an honest chance to grab the American dream that they had all given up so much for. It's really a remarkable story of kindness, loyalty and success. It was sort of a County Galway, Ireland wormhole to Jersey City, New Jersey. Finding familiar faces in their new country had to have been an antidote to the upset and trauma of emigration.

But I am getting ahead of myself; back to the Kellys. I went to Ireland thinking that my great grandparents were Jersey City Patrick Kelly and his wife, Delia Burke Kelly.

Get this. It turned out that there were also two Delia Burkes as well as two Joe Kellys in my family. One of the Delias was married to Jersey Patrick Kelly and the other Delia Burke lived in Manhattan. The Manhattan Delia was from my grandmother's family and for a time I thought she might have been my grandmother. Who wouldn't be confused?

Lorraine had posted pictures of Patrick and Delia Kelly. Honest to God pictures. I thought I was finally looking upon the faces of my great grandparents. I can't tell you how moving and touching it was for me. I stared at the pictures and memorized every line in their faces. Can people imprint on photographs? I think that's what I did. I am still very fond of Patrick and Delia Burke Kelly. They will always have my heart.

This genealogy stuff is hard. There's such a big learning curve to success. As I write this, I'm mindful that my confused thoughts seem to be a common theme. Mistakes are just part of the process. However it is still embarrassing to admit all of my errors in print. It was only by the grace of God, the support of my new cousins, and Louis, that I got anywhere at all.

Anyway, back to just driving around with the photo of the family farm. Amazingly, any grace that was bestowed on me led me right home, sort of like a homing pigeon returning. I actually found the farm! The car took me right there. I didn't know it at the time though. Good grief. How crazy is that? I still really can't believe that happened.

I took a bunch of pictures of the cottage, in part to show Lorraine that her picture really helped, and in part because I thought it was so beautiful.

Then I accidentally drove into town. Where everything would change for me and where I would get precious gifts.

The Kelly cottage on the old Kelly farm, Menlough, Ireland.
It was built sometime during the 1800s.

Photo courtesy of Arthur and Cheryl Kelly

I am using the word "town" loosely to describe Menlough. It is a tiny place – a post office, church, a war memorial, a cemetery, a little food shop and a couple of closed bars. I went into the food store and found the oldest person I could – a guy named Jack. He was an old farmer with muddy boots and a smile that could light up the sky. I asked him if he knew where the old Kelly farm might be.

"Why? Are ye a Kelly?"

Am I a Kelly?

I had never ever considered myself like that nor identified myself that way. I began to babble. "Ummm ummm uh, yeah, I am a Kelly. Joe Kelly is my grandfather. He's the son of Patrick and Delia Burke Kelly, who is the son of Michael Kelly, who is the son of James Kelly and Nancy Carroll." (Maybe I threw in Gimli son of Gloin? I don't remember.)

When I finished boring him to death, I stood there immobile and silent. I had just identified myself as a Kelly for the first time. The axis on which I was spinning tilted a bit. Something huge had just happened. I was rocking my own little world. And I was aware enough to know it.

I was a becoming a Kelly!

I know I must sound like a teenager writing a horribly melodramatic, end of the world poem, but I honestly did somehow feel connected to that place then. Had I really just returned home? Heck, it was only just a few months ago that I was even mildly aware that the Kelly families were relatives. What on earth was happening to me? What was I even doing here?

Jack immediately took my hand and started shaking it around

to those in the store. He began to shout, "I'm shakin ta hand of a woman wit Hubert Kelly's blood running tru her!" Hubert Kelly? Hubert? I recognized the name as a brother or uncle or something to one of my great-great-grandfathers. Or something. I couldn't say for sure which one, though. I thought there might even have been a couple of Hubert Kellys.

Jack announced that I was going to take him to the post office. I was? I was! The storekeeper questioned him about whether it was wise to go off with a stranger. And one from America at that. He walked away from his shopping cart and grabbed my hand. I saw he had some ice cream in his cart. The Irish eat ice cream too? Did he want me to put it away for him, I asked. "No!" he barked "I'm having an adventure now and don't want to stop to put groceries away!" Okay then. As we left, I think the shopkeeper gave me the side-eye stink-eye look. I took it to mean that I had better bring this sweet old farmer back in one piece. I would.

I was thinking that we were going to go far. The drive to the post office took less than twenty five seconds. Jack blasted his way through the door and bellowed to the post mistress, "Guess who I have here? Ye can't guess? I'm going ta tell you then. It's Robin Kelly from America. She has Hubert Kelly's blood flowing tru her."

Good grief, I thought. I really had to find out why Hubert Kelly was like a rock star in this place. I felt uncomfortable with my ignorance.

The post mistress was sweet to Jack and me. She even took our picture. More important, she gave me directions to the Kelly farm. Only one Kelly family was still there, she said – Arthur and his wife Cheryl. She gave me directions to the exact same cottage I had just come from. I honestly couldn't believe it and was secretly thrilled about that as I had felt so comfortable there.

I began to think that a heart hole is maybe like a family GPS, always heading for home?

Jack said we had to leave. "If I don't get home, my son will worry and get all upset with ye." Upset with me? Oh boy. But before we returned to the store, he took me across the street to see the stone that served as the Menlough war memorial. On it were the names of the Kellys who had fought in the war of independence from the British. One of the Hubert's wife's people was on there, too. Ruane. And another's Hubert's wife's people were there too. Potter.

Patrick and Timothy Gavin were on the stone, too. I wondered if they were related to Winifred Gavin, who I would eventually learn was my great-great-grandmother. Jack insisted that I tell him I understood and appreciated all that every man on that memorial had done, in part for me. I did. I really did. It was honestly one of the most touching parts of the trip for me.

Jack got out of my rental car, which was now a hot mess from his muddy Wellies and pants. He went into the store, paid for his drippy ice cream and drove off. I was stunned and felt like I had been in a movie. This lovely, sweet character had grabbed me for an adventure and taught me about local and national Irish history. How on earth did I find this angel of a man? Again, the finger of Goad was all over this trip. I never saw Jack again but still think of him- always with a smile on my face.

Jack had told me which house the Kellys now live in. It was almost dark and rainy by then, but I found it. It is beautiful. I debated whether to knock on the door as I had a bedraggled look to me. I decided that I had to as I had come so far, I just had to try. As I walked up the driveway, the cutest little toddler opened the door and ran outside. She saw me and then, with a horrified look, ran back in and slammed the door. Smart child. I knocked and a beautiful, blond woman opened the door. The little girl was peering at me from behind her mother's legs.

I asked if this was the Kelly home. It was. Then I rambled for a while about Jack, about coming from America, about trying to find the Kelly family. Maybe she could tell I was trying to find my soul center too?

All she said was, "So yer Arthur's cousin? Then ya need ta come in."

Come in? She's inviting a stranger into her home? When she's clearly home alone with her 3 year old daughter and 5 year old son. I'm from New York. We don't do that in New York. Ever. Apparently they do that in Ireland though. How sweet is this country? This woman?

She told me that Arthur was working but he'd be off on Friday. Maybe I'd want to stop by and talk more to him? Did she just fill up her husband's day off with an unannounced visit from an unbeknownst cousin? She did! I accepted in a nano second.

I had just met my first Irish Kelly cousins. What a life! What a world! What a soul rocking moment.

I did a thousand amazing things before I returned to meet Arthur, but they're all irrelevant to this story. On Friday, I went back to meet Arthur. My Irish cousin Arthur.

My cousin...

Arthur was just as lovely and charming as Cheryl. I looked at him and was a little stunned to see that he resembled my youngest son, Zack – tall, lanky, dark hair and handsome. He was also very welcoming.

He showed me pictures of the ancestors and his family tree. He showed me the old part of the farm where the Kelly cottage had been. That cottage had been demolished and the foundation used for part of the existing barn. I had taken pictures of the twin cottage, the Burke cottage – the one I accidentally found before meeting Jack. The two cottages had been just across the lawn from each other, they were exactly the same. I wondered if Delia Burke, my un-grandmother, was a Burke from the Burke cottage. Did she and Patrick really grow up just seventy-five feet apart? That's on my future research list, or maybe Lorraine will take that one as they aren't really my great-grandparents. They're hers.

Arthur is an engineer, but he keeps a few cows. I had Irish Kelly cow cousins. Awwww. He rents out most of his land to a sheep farmer, a friendly guy who grabbed my hand and said, "It's an honor ta shake the hand of a person with Hubert Kelly's blood flowing tru her." The blood of Hubert Kelly again! I explained how Jack the farmer had said the same thing and asked why Hubert was so revered. Did they look at me like I had just offended them? For a nanosecond maybe? I'm not sure.

They explained that when the British took over Irish farms and "allowed" the Irish to be tenant farmers and rent extremely small pieces of their own farms, Hubert got the coveted, yet thankless job of being the local overseer of the biggest farm around. It was Hubert's job to keep the British owner happy and keep goods and money flowing back to England, while still being fair and honest with his own family, friends and neighbors. From what I can tell, Hubert did all of that, was all of that and was revered for being a good, good man in hard, desperate times.

After the British left, Hubert was given the option of buying the entire farm, but as he couldn't pay the taxes on all of it, he chose the portion where the Kelly and Burke cottages sit. The beating heart of the Kelly family.

Arthur explained that Hubert is the only person in the Caltra Catholic Church to be buried adjacent to the church, not in the cemetery. It is as close as he could get to the altar and maybe still be able to hear the singing. It is a high honor.

I found myself proud and grateful that Hubert's blood was flowing through me, too.

I was indeed becoming a Kelly.

Arthur and Cheryl let me take a little stone from the old loo (a new word to me). It was the only foundation left that I knew for sure that my Kelly ancestors had touched back in the day. They shared a baffled look between each other after I asked for a small stone, but they agreed and let me take a tiny stone to bring home. I am an artist and have an old, rusty antique bed spring bolted to my back porch where I put precious things (It's really not as stupid as it sounds). The loo rock went right up. To this day I still look at it and touch it. And remember... I will always remember.

Hubert Kelly
The very good man and the Menlough 'rock star'
Photo courtesy of Arthur and Cheryl Kelly

Cheryl let me grab a few rose hips from a bright pink rose bush on the side of the Burke cottage. My hope was to bring them home and grow Kelly rose bushes for my sisters and new American Kelly cousins. How cool would that be? I froze them for months, planted them, soaked them in warm water, prayed, hoped for a sign of life. Unfortunately, my horticultural skills were completely deficient. It took me more than a year to give up trying to make those dead things grow.

When I left the sacred place that I can now call home, I found myself thinking about how this simple, hard-working (and fertile) farm family got blasted throughout the world like a piñata bursting apart, with each little piece of treasure landing on different continents and in new countries.

Like so many Irish families famine, severe poverty and centuries of traumatic oppression and violence have left their marks on every Irish soul. I believe it gets into the DNA. How desperate must these people have been that they felt their only option for survival was to leave their families, their friends, their country? They had to know that once they left it was unlikely that they'd ever return. That's even if they survived the harrowing trip to their destination.

The emigrating Irish were put in the steerage part of the ships where the livestock went. There wasn't enough food, fresh water, sanitation or sunlight. The ships were called *Coffin Ships* because so many didn't survive the trip. The dead bodies were just tossed overboard. For the ones who did survive, they often arrived at their destination disease-ridden and starving.

I'd like to think that the Kelly ancestors left with hope in their hearts that maybe they really could find a better life. And find jobs and have enough food. Maybe that hope sustained them during the dark and deadly voyage? Thank God for me that they did survive. I struggled to imagine the emotional and physical pain these ancestors endured. I doubt that I would have had that kind of courage and tenacity. Thank God for me though that my ancestors did. Their survival seems Darwinian to me.

I found myself taking one last look at this farm and imagining those large families living in that tiny cottage and working this farm, this big land. The Burke cottage had been abandoned and empty for a long time. It was as if the family just walked out for a bit and never came home. There were still shoes on the floor and on the mantle. I wondered about the second and third level grandparents who loved and worked on the very farm land that I was walking on.

Sacred ground for me and my Kelly family.

The cottage had only two rooms. How could so many people fit in there? When did James and Nancy even have the privacy to make so many kids?

Did they see the warning signs of the upcoming Great Famine/Great Hunger in the 1840s that would devastate the Kelly family, along with millions of other Irish families?

Could James and Nancy have even considered the possibility that so many of their grandchildren would have been pretty much forced to leave their beautiful Ireland to avoid starvation and survive above a subsistence level? This type of poverty and oppression had been going on for nearly 700 years then.

Benjamin Franklin visited Ireland in 1771 and was appalled at the level of abject poverty. He reported to a friend, "The people in that unhappy country, are in a most wretched situation". "They live in wretched hovels of mud and straw, are clothed in rags, and subsist chiefly on potatoes". "Perhaps three-fourths of the inhabitants are in this situation." Franklin blamed the dire situation on the rigid trade restrictions and laws of England. The laws horribly impacted both the Irish population and economy. Franklin feared the same thing might happen in America if the Americans were not freed from British rule. Like America, Ireland was a British colony.

Could Nancy and James Kelly have even considered the possibility that so many Kellys would end up in faraway continents never to be seen again. Kellys like my great-grandfather Michael Kelly (Son of their son Patrick) and my un-grandfather Patrick (also their grandson). Could they have known that this unavoidable mass family emigration of disaster would force their heirs to lose touch with one another and lose the family? Lose the family history. It is still an almost unspeakable horror.

From Colleen Kelly's family tree (more about her later), I would learn that some of the Kellys even ended up in Australia. I presume they may have wound up there on "convict ships" or maybe took advantage of offers to settle in Australia (in an attempt to make room for British citizens in Ireland). After the American war for independence was over, England had to find a new place to dump their convicts instead of sending them to America. Over the course of nearly a century, from 1781 to 1853, England shipped about 26,500 convicts to Australia. Many of their crimes were trivial – stealing food or public drunkenness, for example. After serving their sentences, most stayed in Australia and started new lives as there was no way that they could ever afford to pay for passage back home to

Ireland. They were pretty much forced to start new lives and new roots.

And they were lost to the rest of their families.

Like so many other Irish families, the Kelly family would shatter apart like a piece of precious Irish Waterford crystal falling on to a rock.

The causes of the famine were both biological and political. There was, indeed, a blight that devastated the potato crop. Potatoes were a staple of the poor Irish. The Irish were pretty much forced to become dependent on only one crop, because it was the only crop that could possibly have a chance to be able to sustain an Irish family on the tiny plots of land that the British overseers rented to people. Potatoes give a big bang for the buck in terms of yielding a large-ish crop from a small piece of land. It could sort of- sometimes- maybe feed a family for a year.

There had been another famine in Ireland in 1782–83. That famine wasn't as devastating because the Irish ports were closed to keep the crops and goods in Ireland so people wouldn't starve. It was a strategy that worked. It is stunning that they didn't do that for the next famine also.

During the Great Famine of the 1840s, though, the British Parliament continued to export most of Ireland's crops out of the country, leaving the Irish to starve or being forced to emigrate to avoid starvation.That, combined with the potato blight caused a million people to starve to death and a million more to leave their homeland. Between death and emigration, 25 percent of the population was gone! That percentage is a stupefying number to even fathom. Starving to death is a horrifying way to die. I can't even imagine what it must have been like for parents to watch their children slowly starve and die and not be able to offer comfort or a piece of bread. Wouldn't we all chose to take any pain from our children? It's unimaginable. It was a devastating trauma, horror and humanitarian disaster. Some say it was Irish genocide. It was not unlike the Holocaust or the treatment of Native Americans by colonists. Why does this happen over and over throughout history?

Did my ancestors have the luxury of enjoying their beautiful farm? Each other? Their children? Or was life under British rule a matter of mere subsistence? I know Hubert did a lot to care for everyone but, damn, things must have been dire.

Yet there is a very cozy, sweet feel to the farm now. It should have been a lovely place to grow up. It seemed like Irish paradise to me, but I'm not sure that's how I would have felt in the 1800s. My poor, poor ancestors.

How did the child of an illegitimate Kelly orphan even wind up her? Where it all started? Feeling a reverence and sorrow never felt or even imagined before. Coming from a deep unknown place in my own heart.

As moving as all of this was for me, I couldn't help but miss my mom. She had tried her whole life to find out something – anything – about her family of origin. She died without learning one true thing. And here I was on the Kelly farm with some of my Irish Kelly cousins and a Kelly loo rock in my pocket. She should have been with me. Maybe she was? I'd like to think that maybe a ghost/angel mother was tagging along. Maybe having a ghost whiskey toast? I have to admit that, during this trip, I became a bit of an Irish whiskey aficionado. To be honest, I still am.

Arthur had arranged for me to meet with Father Vincent of the Caltra Catholic Church. Caltra is the epicenter of the Kelly family. What a lovely, kind man he is. He helped me try to find birth, marriage and christening records of my Patrick and Delia Kelly's parents;. I turned up nothing on the "un-grandparents," but spending time with Father Vincent as he was blowing dust off the old, old records was such a treat. He also taught me how to access Irish Catholic records online.

Father Vincent wasn't the only priest I spent time with. I visited Father Reynolds at the Ahascragh Catholic Church on behalf of my cousin Pattie from Oregon. She asked me to look for her third great grandmother's records, Catherine Donnellan. I was also going to look for my own third great grandmother, Nancy Carroll, who was also from Ahascragh (James Kelly's wife). They had to have known of each other as it is such a small town. I am sure that's how Pattie from Oregon and I were connected, as well as cousin Mary Ellen from Washington. Her people are from there too.

But Father Reynolds told me there were no records. The British had destroyed them. "The British didn't care about the names and birth dates of the Irish," he said. "They looked at the Irish as sub-human. Dehumanizing people is the first step toward prejudice and discrimination. Do people keep written records of their sheep and cows' birth dates?" I was stunned.

He was talking about my ancestors. I think he saw how dark the mood had become. Learning about Irish history was often like a punch in the stomach for me.

Father Reynolds then put me in touch with one of Pattie's cousins, Brendan Donnellan, a sheep farmer with a huge farm in Ahascragh. He placed a call to Brendan because, he said Brendan was a man who knew "everything about local families and their histories". He has even written books on Irish history and Irish families.

While we were waiting for Brendan to call back, Father Reynolds grilled me about the election of our new president. He also wanted to know why so many Americans have guns, why they have so many guns, and so on. I confessed I had many of those same questions. While I was in Dublin I noticed that the police didn't even carry guns. That's unimaginable for this country. While I was in Ireland there was a murder somewhere. The entire country was stunned and it was all over the radio stations as it was such an unusual occurrence. There are huge cultural differences between Ireland and America.

Brendan called the priest back. Father Reynolds boomed, "Brendan, I got yer cousin here from America. She's fully armed and locked and loaded. I don't tink ye can say no, Brendan! Ye know how Americans are. Ye had better get over here, Brendan! Ye had better get here fast!"

I couldn't stop laughing. When I get laughing real hard, I often lose control. My sisters are like that, too. It makes my kids nuts. It becomes a boogers out of the nose thing, gagging and breathless. I was close but didn't drool or spit in the church.

Brendan came. In addition to being a sheep farmer, he's also a historian of Irish families. He's written a few books. He's a brilliant man. He showed me his family tree, which goes back to the 1200s I think. It covers tables along three walls in his quaint Irish cottage. He's been working on it for decades.

The field in Ahascragh, Ireland where local families were forced to live together in small, tiny patches.

Brendan showed me all around the area. I saw the cathedrals and burial places that had been blasted out by the British. I saw the field where Irish families in Ahascragh had been forced to live, packed in like bees in a hive. Nancy Carrol's family, my family, had to have been forced into that field too. The feeling I had was almost indescribable. I was looking at this bucolic field that was now lovely and Irish green, yet knowing how my family must have suffered and died there was almost overwhelming. He showed me the adjacent brook where the Irish couldn't fish because those fish belonged to Queen Victoria, who was sometimes known in Ireland as The Famine Queen.

I now finally fully realized that the Irish had literally been tortured. My family had been tortured... It almost made my knees buckle. It was such a painful thing to absorb. I had never even considered a word like that to describe my family. Oh my dear Lord. Seeing the exact places where my family were tormented and starved, was a soul shocking experience. I will never, ever be the same. I found myself tearing up for these poor Irish families, whose only crime was poverty and for being Irish. I had never paid much attention to Irish history before because I never knew I was Irish. I have made it my business since then to read a couple of books on Irish history. It is the least I can do to honor the ancestors' memory.

Brendan Donnellan: Irish historian, writer and sheep farmer

Catherine Donnellan, an ancestor of both Pattie and Brendan, had tried to avoid getting on a coffin ship. Twice. Eventually, she and her baby were pretty much finally forced on a ship to America. It was either that or starve. She clearly didn't want to go and delayed it as long as she could. Allegedly she had been some sort of aristocratic person, before the hard times. When she and the baby arrived at the ship though, records indicate that they were both half naked. The British had to clothe them. I felt like crying again when I read that. I still find it hard to fathom that level of poverty, oppression and suffering.

Afterwards, Brendan took me back to his cottage where his wife Catherine had just made biscuits with homemade currant jelly. There were three of them. I took one. Hands down, it was the best food I had in Ireland. I had never had such good bread before then or since then. The jelly was insanely good. I inhaled mine. They offered me another. I tried to be polite, but gave in to the powerful urge for more. No one ate the third one, and Catherine offered it to me. I'm ashamed to say I took it. And devoured it. And would do it again. I knew I'd never ever get the chance to eat anything like that again. I am hoping that she was pleased that someone went so crazy over her culinary skills. That delusional thought still sustains me.

While we were eating, Brendan told me he was well aware of my Kelly family. Remember he was a researcher and author of Irish history and Irish families. He told me that my Kellys were once rulers in that area. Like kings! "They did pretty good," he said, "and mostly kept the peace for about one thousand years." Holy Cow. I never expected to hear that. They were successful though, he explained, because of the Donnellans'-Brandon's own family. "The Donnellans' were the Kellys' strong men. We would go out and fight their battles and quell dissent. Without the Donnellans', the Kellys would have been nothing."

Understood. Fair enough.

After that, I of course had to do a little research on that nugget for sure. Kelly and O'Kelly are the anglicized names for *O'Ceallaigh*. The name can mean bright haired, or troublesome and maybe even linked to the Gaelic *ceall*, meaning church. This descendants of this clan are directly related to the the Kings of Ui Maine of Connacht (Anglicised as Hy Many). This clan was one of the oldest and had one of the biggest kingdoms in Ireland-the Connacht area, about a thousand square miles. It was centered in County Galway, the South Roscommon area- right where the historical heart of my Kelly family is today. And shockingly exactly where Ancestry pinpointed my genealogical origins.

The Kellys were one of the *Four Tribes of Tara*. The four tribes were an alliance of the O'Kellys, O'Regans, O'Connelly and the O'Harts. They all banded together to fight off Viking invasions during the 8th and 9th centuries. According to tradition, the Hill of Tara is where these kings would meet and is referred to as the seat of the High King of Ireland.

The Hill of Tara is on a high hill with panoramic views where one can see for hundreds of miles in all directions. It would be difficult for the Vikings to sneak up on them there. It is a spectacular place. Today one can see the archeological ruins and burial mounds of these old Kings. It is considered one of the most sacred places in Ireland and should be a 'must see' stop for anyone visiting the country. The *Stone of Destiny* is still atop the great hill. Legend has it that it is where the High Kings of Ireland were coronated. The Kelly kings too? Wow. People kiss it for luck and fortune. I was there and honestly couldn't get myself to kiss such a phallic looking stone. I had arrived just as a couple of tourist buses were leaving. I had the entire place to myself for about an hour and a half. What a miraculous gift for me. It's a quiet place, yet somehow pulses with old energy. The ancient history was oozing out of the air there. And hopefully right into my heart.

Here's an example of how one of the Kelly kings influenced Irish history. In the year 1014 King Brian Boru, the High King of Ireland, (one of Ireland's most beloved heroes and whom nearly everyone in Ireland claims descent from) was fighting Viking raiders in The Battle of Clontarf. One of the Kelly chieftains, *Tadhg More O Ceallaigh,* was killed fighting there along side Brian Boru. History tells that he fought bravely and with honor.

The Kelly king thing was something that every one of the Kelly relatives that I spoke with mentioned. Having the High Kings of Ireland as ancestors is a wonderful honor for all of the Kelly descendants, and remains a great source of pride that's been understandably passed down for generations.

My mother was related to the old Kings of Ireland! Along with millions of others, but still it is amazing. Not a bad legacy for an orphan.

This trip had been like taking LSD – a psychedelic symphony of tastes, knowledge, humor, history. I loved every second. I hated to leave this land – a place that now and forever would have a hold on my heart.

I left with Arthur and Cheryl's e-mail. When I got back, I tried hooking up the Kelly cousins I had met on Ancestry on a group email chain. Everyone was telling me so many stories, that it was becoming hard for me to keep it all straight. I quickly realized that the email chain wasn't working. My clan was getting too big. I inadvertently sometimes got things mixed up and attributed the wrong things to the wrong ancestors. I think maybe I had inadvertently upset or offended a couple of cousins?

We decided to start a Kelly Cousin Facebook page instead. Today there are going on two hundred Kelly cousins from all over the world on it, all posting pictures and nuggets of information and history. We all get to see pictures of the ancestors. I look at these pictures with awe and wonder. Finally an orphan daughter getting to see pictures of relatives...

As happy as I am to finally see the faces and know the names of my relatives, there's a sadness that I didn't get to know them throughout my life. I sometimes get almost a little jealous of how connected many of the cousins are to each other and how growing up together created such a strong bond between them. It's like being happy that a friend wins the lottery, yet a little sad and jealous that it wasn't me too? It's a bittersweet honor that I wouldn't change for the world.

Yet oddly I feel like I know them now. Is this yet another orphan move? To insinuate myself into something like this? Or is is real? For me, it feels real and that has to be good enough.

I am touched by so many of my cousins, for example, PJ Mullaney is a man of honor and intellect, just a good, good man. His love and devotion to his deceased father and children is soul-touching.

Grace Kelly, the aunt everyone loves, is maybe the nexus of the family history now? She helps us all figure out the relationships between us, and tells the stories of the elders. A walking, breathing Kelly history encyclopedia. She's not *that* Grace Kelly though. Although the family lore goes that *the* Grace Kelly, who later became the Princess of Monaco, was indeed from the same Kelly branch of the family. I have no clue whether or not that is true as I haven't researched it, *yet*.

Sabrina Kelly is, for sure, the emotional heart of the family, able to feel pain yet still emote love and hope for us all. The one who never surrenders and will be loyal to her family until her dying breath.

Andrea Kelly, the one who loves her husband so much that it almost seems to be a little window into something sacred, and reminds us all that true love is real.

Andrea agreed to be the broker between her dad Mike Kelly and me. Mike has so much history in his head. He keeps sending me snippets of family connections, and he presumes I know what he is talking about. I found myself wanting to be the person he sees me as. He's one of those people who, if he needed a kidney, I'd be the first in line.

I studied the family history and helped start a Kelly Cousin family tree on FamilySearch (Again, that's the free genealogical search site supported by the Church the Latter Day Saints. Anyone can build free trees and get supporting documentation for the tree. It's well worth a look). All of us Kelly cousins are administrators of it and can add to the tree.

There's a most special cousin for me, though – Colleen Kelly. I call her my soul cousin. She has my heart forever. She's next on my *Must Meet* list. She's the brilliant family researcher. Thanks to Colleen, we all learned about the Kelly Bog Man.

Yes, there's a Kelly Bog Man! In Ireland there are boggy places filled with peat. The peat can be burned as fuel. Arthur had asked me if I wanted to touch one of the peat bricks that he had stacked in the barn after he saw me staring at them. Thinking that he had just asked me if I wanted to touch cow manure, I declined the offer with what I guess was an odd look. I caught Arthur and Cheryl look at each other with maybe confusion? Americans.

Anyway, if people or animals fell into a bog and couldn't get out, they would eventually die. They would then become mummified as there is very little oxygen in these bogs. Many of the bog men still have their (red!) hair, clothing and trinkets intact when they are found. Some of the bog men have been in the bogs for 2000–4000 years. Before Christ was born even. They can look pretty darn good for being dead for centuries. Isn't that wild?

Anyway, in 1821, a couple of O'Kellys found the Kelly Bog Man in Gallugh, County Galway (Google Gallugh Bog Man). He was probably another Kelly as he was found at ground zero for the Kellys, near Caltra. In the spirit of entrepreneurs, a couple of them hatched a scheme to make money. They set up a little business whereby they re-buried their Kelly Bog Man, then allowed people to dig up their "own" bog man – for a fee, of course. Then at night they would re-bury the poor soul, only to let someone else dig him up again the next time.

It was a ghoulish thing to do. In 1829, the Royal Irish Academy finally got wind of it and rescued the Kelly Bog Man. He's now resting peacefully in the Irish National Museum in Dublin. He dates back to 470–120 BC. He is, hands down, my favorite relative. The thinking is that perhaps he had a failed attempt at Kelly kingship? Any Kelly that made a challenge to the presiding Kelly king, and lost, could certainly have wound up in a bog as a final resting place. The next time I go to Ireland, I am absolutely going to make a stop at the National Museum in Dublin to pay my respects.

Colleen had also researched twin Kelly infants, Michael John and James Joseph, who died during the Tuam Children's Home scandal. Their mother, Sarah, died around the time of their births in July 1940. Their father, Hubert (another Hubert) was sickly. The grandmother Julia, tried to get custody of the twins, but was denied because of her age. They were then placed in the Tuam Children's Home. Baby Michael died a month later, in August 1940. Baby James died in September 1940.

Nearly eight hundred children died at the Tuam Children's Home. Many of the dead children were just stored in an underground structure, which was divided into about twenty chambers. Part of the structure had once been a septic tank.

It is one of the darkest times in recent Irish history.

The Kelly family recovered their babies' bodies and reburied them in the Caltra Catholic Church Cemetery. They are now resting with their parents and grandmother there. And near Hubert. The next time I go to Ireland, I will put flowers on their graves for sure.

These stories make me feel rooted to this family. These were real people with real lives and tragedies. After hearing their stories, I began feeling a whole lot less orphany and very connected to this Kelly family.

Then the really big thing happened. Mariah happened.

She popped up on my Ancestry cousin list, but she was no cousin. Mariah wound up being my mother's half-sister. Her father was Joe Kelly! The New York City Joe Kelly, not the Jersey City Joe Kelly.

Her centimorgan count was exactly where a half-aunt would be. And the two other cousins' centimorgan counts were exactly where half-first cousins would be. Mariah was aware of them and knew she was related to them through her other half siblings. She knew she was their half aunt. My centimorgan count with her was in the same range as the other cousins were with her.

Joe Kelly, without a doubt, was my grandfather! New York City Joe Kelly. This time I had the right one. I had found my grandfather!

I couldn't believe I had talked to one of my orphan mother's siblings. Oh my God! My mother had siblings! I had a half-aunt! I was literally shaking. I thought I was having a seizure or something. It was just my known world cracking apart into little mini universes.

Mariah is forty something years younger than my mother. She's younger than I am even. It was mind blowing in so many ways. She didn't seem to know much about the Kelly side of the family and seemed happy to jump into the Facebook group.

She is gorgeous, as are her three daughters, all of whom had either gotten married, engaged or had a baby within a single year. Mariah says that she talks to them all almost every day. She sounds like a wonderful parent. She brought to mind what sweet, loving and patient parents Arthur and Cheryl Kelly are also. This latest generation of Kellys seem like good, solid folks. Maybe the newest Kelly generation might not have to be as burdened with trauma and desperation? I sure hope so.

My mother spent a lifetime trying to learn even a little speck about herself and her family, and her daughter winds up seeing the family farm, talking to her sister and looking upon the face of her father. It's an honor for me, but I wish it were an honor she could have known. I sure hope she's watching.

It was odd to know so much now about the man I thought was my grandfather and his people, yet know exactly zero about the other side of the family.

It was time to find my grandmother.

Joseph Kelly, the author's grandfather, circa 1930–32.

11

TERRORISTS AND SWINDLERS

(Not Everyone Wants New Relatives)

JOE KELLY WAS MY GRANDFATHER.

Even writing that feels surreal. Still. In my heart, I just can't believe we found my grandfather. I never thought I'd find him. I thought maybe I'd just find my grandmother, only if I got really lucky. I was thrilled, but so very sad that my mother couldn't be here to share this unbelievable news. She could have died much happier knowing that half of her life-long quest was fulfilled and maybe half of her heart hole healed?

I spoke with some relatives about Joe. I heard about both the good and the bad about him – he did some wonderful and brilliant things, but he also did some despicable things. But those stories are not mine to tell. It would be unfair to share them in this book. This is my mother's story, and neither she nor I ever even met Joe Kelly.

Joe made and left three (maybe four) families, including my mother, before choosing to settle down with an honest-to-God princess. He had eight (maybe nine) children, including my mother. My mother still has living half siblings. My mother has been dead for twenty-eight years, and she still has half siblings! Is this a crazy world or what? Some are younger than I am. Joe was certainly a fertile guy. All of those years of yearning for a sibling and my mom winds up having had seven (or eight) of them. It would have been such a thrill for her to have met them.

Anyway, the princess. A couple of my new-found relatives mentioned her. I was able to glean the following information from the internet. I presume (and hope) it's accurate, or at least mostly accurate. Her name was Frances Georgette Moss. She was an American. She married Gaston VIII Ross de Galard de Bearn, Prince de Chalais of France. They had a son, the Prince Gaston XIV de Galarde de Bearn, Prince of Viana.

The DeBearn family was from France, and their history goes back to the Crusades. Gaston IV, the Viscount of Bearn (1090–1131) fought in the first Crusade. It is said that he was the first crusader to enter Jerusalem in 1099. It sounds as if he was one of the more enlightened crusaders, and he tried hard to stop the slaughter of Muslims through negotiation. He was not, in the end, successful though.

From what I've heard from family members, the Princess actually left her Prince for Joe Kelly. There was scandal involved (Of course!). Interestingly there's very little reference to it online. I found mention of only one article in a Philadelphia paper, but when I tried to find it and read it, that page was mysteriously missing. One of the relatives swears that the government "wiped him from the internet." Maybe so. He did supposedly do secret work for the government. Is that how these things even work?

Anyway, Joe Kelly became the informal stepfather to Gaston De Bearn XIV, Prince of Viana.

The Prince Gaston De Bearn XIV wound up being an attorney who was close to and collaborated with Robert Kennedy as an intern on the Kefauver Committee, which investigated corruption. He sounds like a remarkable man. I wish I had known him.

I heard a very touching story about how Gaston – that he later tracked Joe down in Long Island, New York when Joe was elderly, alone, poor and sick. Maybe Joe had burned some bridges with other family members? It was Gaston who brought Joe back to Prince William County, Virginia, and took care of him until he died. I've heard that Joe's burial site is in a most beautiful and peaceful cemetery. It seems like Gaston was very kind and generous with Joe's end of life needs. I haven't yet been to the cemetery to see for myself.

Years later, Joe's name was mentioned in Gaston's own obituary. Gaston's devotion to Joe Kelly suggests that maybe Joe figured out how to be a good stepfather?

Back to my mother's story, and mine. I've met quite a few relatives during this search, and each has been an incredible connection for me. It's like being in a dream and remembering it clearly in the morning. Hearing the voices and looking at the faces of the new generation of Kellys is like being in a time machine that allows me to go back and recapture the essence of a family lost. These are my people; my mother's people. Their DNA flows through my veins, too. They are my blood. It is thrilling for the daughter of an orphan to see the faces of family. Finally.

But not everyone was thrilled to meet *me*. In fact, there has been upset.

Pretty big upset.

One relative was so upset that they (gender deliberately not identified here by using the word "they" instead of "he" or "she") decided I was a nefarious and dangerous person. We had spoken on the phone and had what I thought was a nice conversation. What did I know though? Obviously not enough. They actually turned me in for felony crimes to the District Attorney's office in Orange County, New York. That's where I live and work, often with lawyers from that very office. My relative told the DA that I am a person of suspicious nature with possible ties to Islamic terrorists. Islamic Terrorism?! Where the heck did that come from? Plus, they alleged that I am a swindler of inheritances of the Kelly dynasty lands in the beautiful Emerald Isles! Good grief. Who does that happen to!?

I had been asked by them to send a picture of my mother, which is how this person got my email address. I was happy to send a picture. I had hoped that they might send me a picture too. It could have been very lovely.

Here's an excerpt of the email this person then sent to me. I deleted some information that could identify other family members. The misspellings and typos are the writer's; not mine.

This is to advise you that the message that you left on the answering machine on February 14m was saved. This is to further advise you that when I responded to your message and you answered, our conversation was listened to and recorded by the person with whom I share my present residency.

Furthermore, today I reported you to the Orange County District Attorney as someone of a suspicious nature with motivations that may be combined with ... who had become a member of the

*Islamic philosopju wotj hatred amutjomg of a Christian nature
and/or those who profess to believe in Jesus Chris ... who may
be in cahoots with you to abscond with my inheritance of the
property ofrom whwned by my Kelly family family for hundreds
of years and that you took the time to go and view the property,
a total stranger to the family with possible ulterior, calculating
motivations ...*

*I also told the DA how you tried to question me about the names
of other members of the Kelly dynasty which you were missing in
order to further stake your claim to the property which you and ...
so covet.*

All good things from me to you.

Wow, right? I took great comfort that the conversation may have
been recorded, as it would prove that we never spoke of money,
terrorism or swindling. During the conversation it was clear that
they didn't believe in DNA science and thought it was a hoax.
OK. I never tried to convince anyone of anything. I just wanted
to say hello and maybe get some genealogical information. I felt
honored at the time to be talking to one who would have, should
have, known my mother. The honor certainly wasn't mutual. I
did actually get confirmation of the names of Joe's parents. I had
already gotten that from Mariah though, so I didn't learn anything new. I guess that's the part of the conversation that somehow became transformed into me trying to stake a claim on the
Kelly dynasty in Ireland? Who knows?

But it turns out that this bizarre accusation actually interfered
with my job for a short time. I am part of a team that includes the
police, child welfare investigators, assistant district attorneys,
mental health professionals and county attorneys. The team in-
vestigates allegations of felony assaults against children, sexual

abuse and rape of children as well as the murder of children. I work with them all of the time. For a while, as a result of this relative's complaints, those who worked in the district attorney's office were not permitted to communicate with me as I was then being investigated as a person of suspicion for terrorism and swindling. Wow. They couldn't talk to me or return my messages. Although I understood their actions, it was embarrassing for me. It actually stopped me me from doing part of my job for a while as this meant I could not accompany the children I was trying to help when they had to give grand jury testimony against their abuser. It was a big deal to the children. I wound up meeting them afterwards for ice cream or donuts. It wasn't the same level of support by any means.

I will admit, though, that I did take a little advantage of the situation. As I had never before – or since – been investigated for ties to Islamic terrorism, I wasn't sure what to expect. I got it into my head, though, that maybe a SWAT team would search and ransack my house in the middle of the night looking for weapons of mass destruction or ... something else terroristy.

Who would really know that stuff anyway? Other than an actual terrorist.

Anyway, my two sons had recently moved back home and, like a lot of sons, they are not all that neat and tidy. One of them, Max, is a woodworker, and there were always wood chips on the floor. Cleaning up wood chips is like trying to control the hairy mess when huskies shed. After the terrorism allegations, I kept nagging and telling them they had to keep the house perfectly clean so when the authorities come to toss the house, in the wee hours of the morning, I won't be more embarrassed than I need to be.

I also made sure that I looked neat and tidy when I went to bed.

No messy bed head for me in case I had to have a mug shot taken. I didn't want to have bed hair for such an important picture. I wanted to be as ready and dignified as possible for a troop of federal officers in the middle of the night. Although my sons thought I was ridiculous, the house never looked better. I was almost sad that I told them when it was over.

I was eventually told that the case against me was closed because the complainant was not willing to give their own name, address, or other identifying information. People are apparently not allowed to make anonymous complaints of felony crimes.

One lawyer mentioned I could even sue this person for defamation. I could certainly make a case for emotional distress. I really was upset.

I honestly can't say that I was cleared of terrorism charges, though- they were just dropped.

I would have preferred a formal certificate or declaration that said, "It has been decreed that Robin is not a terrorist or a swindler." That would have been a nice thing to display, right? We should all have something like that just in case of a fabricated felony terrorism allegation emergency.

The sad thing is that my sisters and I would have helped this person. We heard there were financial issues. How could we not want to help a relative of our mother's? Our mother would have certainly done so. At this point though, they are too dangerous for us to have further contact.

No one told me that in the pursuit of finishing my mother's quest and finding her parents, that I could be reported as a terrorist and a swindler. That absolutely was not in any genealogy guide book.

All kidding aside, this weird reaction to hearing from a long-lost relative (and some mild, passive negative reactions from just a couple of others) made me realize that not everyone really wants new relatives. Some new cousins wanted to talk to me in person, others just wanted to email for a bit. Others text. I have contact with some a few times a month, others want no contact at all.

That's all totally fair and fine.

My goal is not to force anyone to accept me, I am just searching for the truth. The truth of my family.

But I have to say that the vast majority of my new relatives have been some of the most welcoming, encouraging, compassionate people I've ever met in my entire life. They are the ones who *Give a Cup of Kindness*, over and over.

This quest has taken me to sacred Native American caves in the high desert of Oregon, the rainforests of Washington State, the North Atlantic Sea in Ireland, the bogs and barns of County Galway, Ireland, New York City, Jersey City. The places that I've been to have been amazing, but it's the people I've met, who have touched my hart and soul forever.

It's been such an honor to meet them all.

Well … maybe one of them, not so much.

12

KELLYS HERE, KELLYS THERE, KELLYS EVERYWHERE

THROUGH MARIAH AND OTHER FAMILY members, I finally realized that I had the wrong Joe Kelly. I was not a Jersey City Joe Kelly granddaughter, but a Manhattan Joe Kelly granddaughter. Thank goodness for me that the Joes were cousins, and that my trip to Ireland was still valid in terms of being with the right family and the same farm.

I look back at my basic confusion and feel like a kid learning to ride a bike without the training wheels for the first time. Kids ride along believing that their parent is still running behind them and holding them steady, never realizing that they are riding the bike alone. I had somehow managed to wobble off on my own in the right direction and, incredibly, arrived at the right destination. They say God watches over fools. I can't argue with that.

After I got back from Ireland, Louis took me back to one of our hottest date places – back to the New York City Municipal Archives on the Lower East Side of Manhattan. Ahhh, he really knows how to treat a girl.

Another blessing in this story is that everything in my mother's history seems to have happened in New York City. Louis lives in the city and was in the area daily. I was going down a few times a month. If I had been living anywhere else, the research would have been nearly impossible. At the very least I would have had to hire someone to go through the film records. I doubt that a hired helper would have looked as hard as we did and found so much unexpected information.

I would later realize that there is so much more information in original documents than ever gets uploaded onto public records and internet genealogy search sites. It was this hidden information that would ultimately prove most crucial. I am a huge believer in the necessity of getting copies of original documents. A suggestion to these DNA companies would be to offer a way to order copies of original certificates from their sites. I believe people would be willing to spend the extra money. I would. I have uploaded and shared everything we've found. I want it to be as easy as possible for any other family members looking for documentation.

Anyway, my grandfather Joe Kelly's parents were Michael J. Kelly and Maria (pronounced Mariah) Dowling Kelly. I came to find out that Joe was the second youngest of six living kids. We actually found two additional children, one who died as an infant and the other who died as a toddler, Winifred and baby Michael. Michael died of tubercular meningitis at about a year old, and Winifred died at age three or four of bronchial pneumonia with a contributing factor of general weakness. These wee ones never made it to a census, which is how I came to appreciate the necessity of researching and getting the original documents. If I went only by census records, I would never have known about the poor missing Kellys. For the longest time I thought that Joe was the baby of the family. We accidentally found a brother who was 5 years younger than Joe – Harry Kelly.

I find myself a little contented to know that because baby Michael and Winifred Kelly are mentioned in this book, they will no longer be forever forgotten. They were real babies that mattered to their family. They never got to grow up and do anything special. But they mattered. And still do.

After discovering their deaths, I was thinking about how one would even recover, much less survive the loss of two children. Two children! Babies that the Kellys had to have fallen in love with before they died. How does one even go on? Are we just big babies now? Were our ancestors tougher? Colder? Or just more inured to trauma and tragedy as it was so much more prevalent?

Michael and Maria were two parents who had left their own families, countries and old life to start over in a new country. A new country that wasn't always welcoming to the Irish, where in fact there was a lot of prejudice and discrimination toward the Irish. Advertisements for job openings often included the words "No Irish." In England there were signs that said, "No Irish, No Blacks, No Dogs." In America the Irish were depicted in cartoons, stories and articles as somehow being lazy, aggressive, ugly (almost simian like). Irish women were shown as being almost like big, ugly, giant men as contrasted to quaint, petite, beautiful British ladies. These falsehoods contributed to discrimination and prejudice against the Irish. Even Winston Churchill said, "We have always found the Irish a bit odd. They refuse to be English". The sentiment runs deep. *Most Irish interpret that quote as a compliment.*

The discrimination started when England sent over Protestant settlers, mostly from Scotland, into Northern Ireland, displacing the Catholic Irish who were already living there. Ireland had become primarily Catholic after the Romans massacred all of the Druids. The Druids were said to be focused on the rhythms of the natural world, not unlike the Native Americans. And many believe were able to harness some of the natural power and magic of nature.

The settlement of Protestants and the forced displacement of Catholic Irish in a Catholic land, started hundreds of years of oppression, bigotry and conflict. These same prejudicial attitude against the Irish were in America too. Remember that America had been a British colony and absorbed many of the British beliefs, rituals and attitudes.

These were already tough times for the Kellys. Maria and Michael lost two children on top of their mountain of trauma, grief and loss. It is unimaginable.

At the time the Kellys were living in New York City during the late 1800s through the 1920s, they were poor. Dirt poor. They were living in a tenement. The conditions in the tenements at the time were cold and rough. They didn't have access to the sanitation that we have today. The tenements were not big places – maybe 2–3 rooms. At one point the Kellys had up to 8 children, themselves and Maria's brother, Patrick Dowling, living there. There were maybe 11 people living in a tiny cramped tenement!

Michael was a coachman and drove a horse-drawn buggy. Did he know the Jennings brothers back in County Galway? Is that where he learned his horse skills? Sometimes coachmen lived above the stables. There may or may not have been toilets. We tried finding the building, but the records for that side of the street were missing. Generally, the apartments had a wood or wood/coal stove. For anyone with pulmonary issues (like those poor babies), the air would have been compromised. What a choice: freeze to death or exacerbate breathing problems by trying to stay warm.

I have to presume that there may have also been some malnutrition. Feeding six kids is never easy. But for these poor folks in tenements, it could have been extra hard, particularly with just one person working outside of the home. Did Michael feel the pressure of keeping everyone safe, fed and alive? How could he not? How did he manage that? It sounds like bone-breaking poverty. Patrick's salary had to help. The only blessing is that the whole neighborhood was in the same situation. They were by no means the only poor folk on the block.

As I write this, I'm picturing the smoggy, dirty, cramped and impoverished area of one of the world's greatest cities, and I find myself wondering if they missed beautiful County Galway. It is one of the prettiest places in Ireland. Vibrant, luminous greens with rolling hills, quaint cottages, big sky. How could they not miss such a beautiful place that had to be in their heart and souls forever? Did memories of home bring them comfort? Or longing and homesickness? Did they regret leaving the Emerald Isles? Or did they still believe that their best hope was in this new country? Or maybe both?

The death records indicate that the wee ones were buried in Calvary Cemetery in Queens. New York. Within a short time, we were able to get copies of Michael's and Maria's death certificates, too. Michael died in 1921 from stomach cancer, and Maria died in 1926 of chronic nephritis. Nephritis is a condition that often starts as a urinary infection that then can cause kidney issues. It's apparently painful in the pelvis and can cause issues with urination, swelling and so on. Poor, poor Maria. By July 1921, she was a widow. Harry was only 14 or 15 years old.

My mother had been born five months earlier than Michael's death. Did Maria or Michael– my mother's grandparents– even know about the baby? Did they ever lay eyes on my mother? Heck, did Joe ever lay eyes on his daughter? Who knows? They certainly couldn't have taken her.

Joe had enlisted in the service in September 1920, three or four months after my mother's conception. Coincidence?

Joe's older sister Katy had married Frank McDonald at age thirty in 1921, just a few weeks before Michael died. Interestingly, in 1925 Katy Kelly McDonald was living back at home with Maria, her brothers James and Robert, and her sister Margaret – and with a son, Eugene. The census said Eugene was eleven, yet she had been married only four years. Where did Eugene come from or go? Was my mother not the first "illegitimate" Kelly baby? Or did the census taker just make a mistake? Was he the child of a Kelly cousin? Who knows? It's an unknown story, but Katy was there in her mother Maria's final days. It had to be comforting to Maria to have some of her kids there when she met her maker.

Michael's and Maria's death certificates say they were buried at Calvary Cemetery in Queens, too. Calvary is the largest cemetery in the United States with more than three million people buried there. That is a big, big cemetery! There are also many celebrities buried there, a couple of whom I had even checked out as possible actress grandmothers: Ethel Barrymore, Irene Dunne and Pola Negroni. That's kind of weird right? Don Corleone is also there.

As Louis lives nearby, he goes with some regularity to visit relatives who are buried there: his paternal grandmother and five of her kids, uncles, aunts and so on. He researched all of the children buried with his grandmother so he could add them to the tombstone. His belief in honoring the ancestors and documenting family history is prominent in his life. I never saw anyone walk with the ancestors like Louis does. I think that's what always attracted me to Native American cultures – the way they revere the ancestors and how the ancestors remain a part of their earthly life.

Anyway, Louis actually found the Kelly plot at Calvary. We had both assumed that it might be an unmarked grave without a tombstone as they seemed so poor. Instead he found a beautiful tombstone that said

In Memory of Our Beloved Parents

Michael Kelly died June 12, 1921

Maria Kelly died April 5, 1926

Rest in Peace

The tombstone had a carved Palm or Lily branch with a cross on it. It is honestly quite lovely. I was at work when Louis texted me the pictures of it. I found it chilling. It was almost disorienting for me as I had never thought much about cemeteries. My reaction really surprised me. We still wonder who paid for that, Robert Kelly? He was the one arranging for Maria's death paperwork.

A month or so later, Louis took me there. I brought some pink geraniums to plant so they'd be blooming all summer. As I was standing there, the thought hit me that I was standing in the exact same spot where Kellys had stood. They had to have been there burying their dead, grieving, sharing tears. And here I was, the unknown Kelly, planting geraniums. The illegitimate Kelly granddaughter, planting geraniums. I wondered if Michael and Maria knew or could tell I was there, or even who I was. I'd like to think it was okay. At the very least, I think they'd be happy to have someone tending the plot.

Naturally thoughts turned to my mother. Michael and Maria were her grandparents. I was standing at the site of my mother's grandparents' grave. The thought just blew me away.

So did the wish that I could be standing there with my mother. Maybe I was?

When we stopped at the cemetery office to get directions to the plot. The Calvary staff casually mentioned that there were seven people in the plot. Seven? Oh wow. I had presumed the babies as well as Maria and Michael would be there, but who else?

Perhaps my grandmother who had possibly died in childbirth while trying to deliver their grandchild? Is that something that the Kellys' would have offered my maternal grandmother's family if she had died giving birth to my mother?

I just had to know.

I paid a hefty fee for them to research who else was in the plot. It was totally worth it. The Calvary research staff said it could take up to three months. Every day I couldn't wait to check the mail. I was like a kid scratching off a lottery ticket. It finally came, almost six months later!

It was totally not what I expected.

There wasn't a missing grandmother.

I was surprised to see that Joe's sister Margaret Kelly was there. Still named Margaret Kelly. Sounds like she may have never married? I wondered why. I also wondered why Margaret was the last one in. She was in her sixties when she died.

There were two other surprises. Two of Maria's older siblings, Patrick and Catherine Dowling, were there with everyone else. Both had also emigrated from Ireland. Wow. I had never even heard of Patrick Dowling at the time I got the records.

I had heard of Catherine Dowling though. She had shown up in the 1930 census as living with Joe Kelly and his family in Rockland County, New York. She died in 1933 at age sixty-nine. Her death certificate said she had died at The little Sisters of the Poor. Her body had been signed out by a Mother Superior. Was Catherine a nun? An ex-nun? That would clear up the mystery of how on earth the Grays found a baby born in New York City. Maybe the story of the foundling hospital nun intervention was true? Oh my goodness, my heart was starting to race again.

I did some research and found that there was, indeed, an Irish immigrant nun named Catherine Dowling. She had been the nun who started the Sisters of Charity in the New York City metropolitan area. They are now located in Rockland County, New York, right near where Joe Kelly and his family had been living while she was staying with them. The Sisters *did* do work with orphans and unwed mothers. Of course, my first thought was that maybe Joe Kelly used his Aunt Catherine Dowling, the nun from Ireland, to help him years ago solve the extra baby problem. Maybe he owed her? Is that why they were taking care of her in her older years?

I was sure this was it. I was sure I had a breakthrough. It was very exciting stuff.

Until it wasn't.

I made contact with a lovely nun researcher from the Sisters of Charity, who was very excited to be in touch with Sister Catherine Dowling's family. Like Hubert Kelly in Menlough, Sister Catherine Dowling was like a rock star there. They had some sort of ceremony every year to honor the sister and commemorate her work. The research nun said that they would love for us to come and be a part of this year's ceremony as they weren't aware of any relatives and would be honored if family could be there. Wow. Heck yeah, I'd come. Proud to. Thrilled to.

But then we started to compare notes.

Their Sister Catherine Dowling came from Limerick, which was about seventy-four miles (115 kilometers) from Menlough, Ireland. That was a huge distance in the 1800s. I was starting to wonder if, again, there were two people with the same name on my search. Then we compared the birth dates of our two Catherine Dowlings. Different. I realized that, of course, there were two Catherine Dowlings, and our Catherine wasn't the big shot nun. Our suspicion now is that she was with the Little Sisters of the Poor because she was a poor, old Irish woman.

It's not known why she was no longer living with Joe Kelly by 1933. Joe had listed himself as a captain of a yacht in the 1930 census. It was probably the yacht he helped build for Adolf Zuker, the man who started Paramount Pictures.

Maria's brother Patrick, also single, died at the age of sixty-five about two years after Michael died. He was living with Maria at the time of his death, too. He also died of pulmonary issues. Catherine, Margaret and Patrick were all single. Why was that? I never found out.

I didn't find my grandmother in the Kelly family plot. Admittedly that was a big disappointment.

But I did find something special. I found my great-grandmother. I learned more about the kind of woman Maria was. I realized that for Maria Kelly, family was everything. For this one dirt-poor, fiercely loyal sister, mother and wife, it was always all about family first. She had survived two children, a brother and a husband, yet she somehow made it clear to her surviving children that her single sibling Catherine could go in the Kelly family plot, too. Pure loyalty. I am feeling proud that, like Hubert Kelly, her blood flows through me, too.

I was not as successful in keeping up with Joe's brothers, Robert, James and Harry. Because their names are so common, it was impossible for me to distinguish them from all of the rest of the gazillion James, Harry and Robert Kellys. There are a couple of lost Kellys to be sure, but at least many of the lost have been found. Maybe one of their grandchildren will read this book so we all can meet more Kelly cousins. If so, I will update the book.

The Kelly family experienced a second wave of disconnection with each other once they reached America. This is in addition to the disconnect with the family left in Ireland. It seems that although they may have landed fairly close to each other in the New York, New Jersey metropolitan area, they may not have maintained contact? There were no phones then. No cars that they'd really have access to. The mail was cumbersome. Visitation was hard and difficult and maybe expensive. None of them had any extra money. I say this because as I found more and more of the cousins, none of them seemed to really know much beyond their immediate family. No one had a sense of the total family picture.

No one was keeping track of everyone.

They were lost to the folks back home and in America.

We all seemed lost to each other too.

13

WORLD WAR II

(The Nexus of Father, Daughter and Future Husband)

MY MOTHER WAS SMART. REALLY smart. I don't think she knew it though. I certainly didn't.

I recall a conversation my sisters and I had as young teens about our parents' intelligence. We were just amazed that three smart kids like us came from two people who seemed a bit ... cognitively limited. There was even some speculation that we, too, might have been adopted because of our superior intelligence. It almost seemed to us that our parents' stupidity and oddness were inversely proportional to our superior intelligence and coolness. How could that even be?

I remember one Mother's Day when my father took us all out to dinner at a Japanese restaurant. I remember it for two reasons.

One, my mother put so much effort into getting us all ready that she forgot to put her own shoes on. She didn't realize she was still wearing her fuzzy slippers until we were in the restaurant. Naturally, I was mortified. Of *course* she forgot to put shoes on. Good grief. How could she possibly be our mother?

Then two, the big thing happened. She began to speak to the waitress. In Japanese! Rather than being impressed that she seemed pretty fluent in Japanese, I was mortified that she was calling attention to herself by not speaking English. Worse, she was calling attention to our entire family. In a pre-adolescent tsunami of narcissism, I demanded she stop that immediately as people were looking at us. I became even more annoyed when she and my father shared a smile over my embarrassment. It wasn't funny at all!

It wasn't until I became the parent of adolescents myself that I was able to put the incident into perspective. I recall smiling when one of my sons suggested I allow him to roll out of a moving car as I was dropping him off at the mall. He didn't want his friends to see me. If they saw me, they'd know he had parents. Apparently, he preferred that they think he was sort of hatched from an egg or raised by wolves. That would have certainly been cooler than having parents.

Or a grandmother who spoke Japanese.

Every once in a while, my mother would talk about her time in the Navy during WWII. She went into the service with the goal of driving a jeep for important people. I presume her role model for a job like that was Kay Summersby, the former model who drove Eisenhower around and got all sorts of medals and awards for her heroism. Who wouldn't want a glamorous job like that?

But the Navy officials gave my mother an intelligence test and decided she was better suited to other things. Things like learning a new language – Japanese – than being a driver for some bigwig. No jeep driving for her. They sent her to school where she learned the language and was trained to intercept and crack Japanese codes. Is that crazy or what?

There is a story about how she wound up intercepting a crucial transmission, almost by accident. Apparently, she transcribed transmissions so much that they became rote to her. Almost kind of boring, in fact. She would turn them in to the powers that be and didn't always pay attention to the specifics of what they said.

After she turned over one submission, the Navy bosses put her in a room and interrogated her. Did she make it up? Is she sure that she recorded it correctly? Was she impaired in anyway? Were her loyalties to the USA? And the Allies? In telling us the story, she said she had honestly been afraid they were going to arrest her for something (something that was not Islamic terrorism). She said that she often didn't even pay much attention to what she decoded because the messages often referred to bearing and heading locations and nautical numbers. She wasn't even sure which interception they were referring to during her interrogation

Barbara Katherine Gray, the author's mother,
who served in the Navy during World War II.

As it turned out, the message she'd intercepted was about ... I don't actually know. She never told us the specifics. I think it was about some sort of impending attack or the location of some big shot Japanese general. Or something. She never gave us the specific details.

What I *do* know is that she inadvertently saved hundreds of lives. How cool and crazy is that? A war hero mother.

When we got her military records, there was a letter saying that she had gotten an award and a letter from the President for her work. But the letter also said she could not ever say anything about the medal or exactly what the award was for because she was in a secret intelligence unit. My mother the spy. She never did tell us anything. One thing she was really, really good at was keeping secrets.

One of the more amazing things about this genealogical story is the number of seemingly impossible coincidences. My mother's father, Joe Kelly, inadvertently played a part in saving my father's life during World War II. It's as if families are all interconnected with invisible tethers that hold us together even through life and death. I've always felt that God shows through coincidences. If I'm right, we are coincidental royalty.

According to a couple of relatives, Joe Kelly helped manage the logistics of arming the Merchant Marine ships in WWII. He parlayed his experience building and repairing big boats and yachts for Adolf Zuker into helping arm the Merchant Marine fleet. It's not clear how he got the job, but it seems to be true. I heard it from a few relatives, although I could not find written reference to it. He even apparently was awarded a Congressional medal for his work. As I am not a legitimate Joe Kelly granddaughter, I was not able to get his military records without perjuring myself. Believe me, that killed me.

Relatives have told me that Joe knew Roosevelt, Joe Kennedy, Richard Nixon, Henry Cabot Lodge II, Fulgencio Batista (the president of Cuba from 1940–1945). One cousin mentioned being with Joe Kelly in a fancy hotel in New York City and running into and talking to Richard Nixon about business. Again, I could find nothing online about any of this, but it sure is a fascinating possibility. A Kelly from people in County Galway playing with the big guys. The real big guys.

Toward the end of WWII, the Merchant Marines were getting annihilated by both the Germans and the Japanese. The enemy troops were trying to stop the Marines from delivering food and supplies to the Allied soldiers. The ships were sitting ducks. The Merchant Marines saw as much action as another branch of the military.

And – coincidence here – my father was a Merchant Marine assigned to the Pacific, Atlantic and Middle East war zones. His fleet was attacked and I recall him saying that about a third of the ships he was with, were sunk in a single day. The ships near my dad went down. His ship didn't. Why? Because the ships were armed and could fight back. They all didn't have to all die that day in that battle. The Merchant Marines gave them hell that day.

William George Gerry, the author's father, Who served in the Merchant Marines during World War II.

In part because of Joe Kelly's work, my father didn't die that day. How crazy is that? Joe helped save the life of a man who would become his lost and forgotten daughter's husband. The father of Joe's own granddaughters. You just can't make this stuff up. None of them ever realized the connection.

I am proud of all three of them and honored that they served their country.

I would be remiss not to mention other Kellys who fought in other wars. The following information was provided by my cousin Colleen Kelly, the family historian. I want to thank them all for their service.

Hubert and Julia Kelly's son PJ Kelly died in Flanders in WWI.

John and Mary Kelly lost another PJ Kelly in WWII.

Mary Elizabeth Kelly (aka Lily), was a nurse in England during WWII.

There are two Michael Kellys and a James and John Kelly named on the Menlough war memorial.

And of course, The Battle of Clontarf. Kelly chieftain, Tadhg More O Ceallaigh, was killed fighting Vikings with Brian Boru.

And all of the other Kelly Kings who fought trying to stop Viking invaders from taking over Ireland.

I'm sure there are many other Kellys who served their country. I'm sorry that I don't know their names so I could acknowledge them here for their sacrifice and service to America and Ireland. I would be happy to include them in future versions of this book.

It is important to keep emphasizing how the invisible grace of God might look to our families.

This book is full of examples of how historical trauma impacted this family. And every other family. In these times most people now understand the impact that Post Traumatic Stress has on the military. Back in the day though they didn't know about it. It used to be called Battle Fatigue or Shell Shock, now it's PTSD. Regardless of what people call it, it has to be worse for families that have such a strong traumatic family history to begin with. Like my poor immigrant family.

14

MY GRANDMOTHER WAS NOT GLORIA SWANSON OR MARY PICKFORD (BUT MAYBE NANCY CARROLL?)

I WAS STUNNED WHEN I learned that Joe Kelly had worked for Adolf Zuker, the guy who started Paramount Pictures. I started to figure that maybe the actress grandmother story might actually be true. Maybe our childhood fantasy hadn't been so far off? Maybe we really did have a rich and famous grandmother? It made perfect sense in Robin, Dawn and Billie Land.

In my search, census records were an important source of information. They were done every ten years but weren't entirely reliable. For example, if Joe had gotten a new job the day after the census taker had been at his home, it might not even show up in the next census. The records indicated that he was a mechanic, a chauffeur, and a captain on a yacht –likely the yacht Joe had helped build for

Zuker's wife Lottie. Was he also Zuker's chauffeur? Was it Joe's job
to drive beautiful actresses back and forth? Oh my my.

That's maybe how my grandparents met? Or maybe Joe's father
Michael was one of the carriage drivers for Zuker? The census
data indicates that Joe's sisters Katy and Margaret made dresses
for a private family. The Zukers? In 1916, Zuker purchased an ar-
mory on 26th Street in Manhattan (not that far from where Joe's
parents lived) and converted it into a movie studio. Holy cow! Joe
could have been around a lot of actresses in any of those capaci-
ties that either he or his family may have worked for Zuker.

I was about to book a trip to the Hollywood sidewalk stars.

Zuker's early films feature actors and actresses called "The
Famous Players Film Company." He formed the group in 1912,
the time of the silent screen movies. It was an era when women
swooned while watching Rudy Valentino (another Famous
Player). Most average folks had never seen anything like a movie.
They were transfixed and transported to a whole new reality. It
would be like us being beamed up by Scotty to a new world and a
new civilization in space, a completely mind-bending experience.
These actors and actresses became almost more than human.

And maybe one of them met up with Joe Kelly in a hot car? These
were the days when most people traveled by horse and carriage.
To have access to a car like Joe did would have been pretty spectacular. Joe Kelly was literally tall, dark and handsome. And
based on family stories, he certainly had a way with women. Who
could resist a hot young man in a hot car?

I decided to check on Ancestry.com to see if any of the movie
stars' family members and I shared DNA. It's possible to compare family trees to see if there's a genetic match with the person

who did the tree. I didn't realize at the time that there are professional genealogists who just do the family trees of movie stars. Naturally, I did not show a genetic connection to any of those pros. I didn't show any connection to any of their family members either. Of course, that could also be explained away if the person doing the tree had married into the family.

I hadn't gotten a new big genealogical hit with DNA in a thousand years. I was running out of options. I felt that trying this way was my only real chance at the time. I had nothing to lose — except a bunch of time.

I decided that my first move was to check the family trees of all the actresses in the Famous Players list.

And I got a hit!

Nancy Carroll. Her real name was Ann Veronica Lahiff. She was a beautiful freckled red head just like my sister! And she looked oddly like my mother and sister, except she was very small. Both Billie and my mother were tall. Nancy fit the bill as she was an Irish actress. She also was working on TV in a series with her own daughter in the 1950s when Jennie Butler was dying.

Remember the deathbed scene when Jennie told my mother that her biological mother had recently been on TV? Nancy was a perfect solution to my stubborn problem. I even sent my sisters a picture of her next to our mom. This had to be it! I felt it in my soul. I just *knew* I had finally found my grandmother.

Until I didn't.

I contacted one of Ann Veronica LaHiff's grandsons. He was absolutely lovely and even open to the possibility that there may have been an illegitimate child. He put me in touch with one of his cousins. She was the family historian/genealogist. She was just as sweet and accommodating as he was. The compassion of strangers on my quest never ceased to astound me and touch my soul.

We exchanged several emails and tried to figure out the connection. I was so touched by her grace. After all, here was this total stranger poking around in her family history. Many people would have blocked me (or maybe turned me in as a terrorist). She had both compassion and curiosity.

After a while, though, we realized that my connection to the Lahiff family was through a man who married into the family. He was some sort of cousin through my father's mother – my British granny. Crazy coincidence, right?

By then though, I had developed an affection for the LaHiff cousin and was disappointed that I wasn't part of her lovely, warm family. I asked if I could be an honorary family member, and she said I could. See? That's kind of an orphan move, I think. Who does that or asks that? Maybe a woman raised by an orphan?

After I blew through the Famous Players, I started a list of *all* the actresses who were working in 1920 (the year my mom was conceived). There were hundreds of them. I started with the clearly Irish actresses. Then the British sounding ones. Then the tall ones (remember my sisters are Vikings). Then I just started going alphabetically. I can't even tell you the hours and hours and weeks I spent on this. It was a snowy, cold winter, so there wasn't much else to do, but I was clearly bordering on obsessive with it. Maybe my sisters were becoming concerned for me, that maybe I was cracking up? They never asked how the search was going.

I ruled actresses out if they were too young; I made an arbitrary cutoff of age fifteen. Joe was nineteen and my hope was that he wouldn't have gone after girls younger than that. Most of the actresses were over sixteen, anyway. I also didn't seriously consider actresses over thirty-five. My assumption was that they would have been savvy enough to ignore Joe's adolescent charms. My other assumption was that any sex that occurred was consensual, largely because I couldn't bear to think otherwise.

I matched with one family member of actress Helen Arnold. She was eleven years older than Joe, though, and she was making movies only from 1916–1918. I figured that between her age and her short stint in the business, she was an unlikely candidate. I also figured that if she were really my grandmother, I'd be related to most of her relatives, not just one.

Another silent movie actress that I was related to was Nellie Bly Baker. I thought she was a real contender too. My uncle was a Nellie Bly baby. Could they be the same person? Oh wow. I was getting a good feeling until I realized that they weren't the same person at all. I came to find out that I was related to Nellie Bly Baker through my dad's mom again, not my maternal grandmother at all. What are the odds?

It's funny that there were 3 actresses connected to my British granny. While I was doing this research, I was contacted by a British TV producer who told me that I was related to some famous actor or actress in the United Kingdom and they were going to do some sort of genealogy show on them. Would I be interested in being on the show? Of course I would be. If for nothing else, just for curiosity. I guess they had enough people though and didn't use me. It's fascinating that acting seems to run in that side of the family. It's probably another DNA thing.

Some of the actresses I was most hopeful about were Billie Burke, the good witch in The Wizard of Oz (who wouldn't want her as an ethereal grandmother?); Talulah Bankhead because I just liked the name Talulah; Yvonne DeCarlo, the best ever potential exotic grandmother; Marlene Dietrich (oh my God!). Going through all of these actresses was sort of like buying a grandmother lottery ticket. You buy the ticket and get to have a fleeting fantasy of what amazing, spectacular thing you're going to do when you win- maybe get a Marlene Dietrich tattoo or something? It was like watching a rock star and imagining running off with him. In the Kelly family, it seems that there are a few of us who would not think twice about walking away with Bono if he asked.

In the end, I went through nearly two hundred and fifty actresses in hopes one of them was my grandmother. I almost finished the alphabet. I finally grew discouraged with my lack of progress when I finished "Y," and I took a break. I never went back to my alphabet search but continued to be plagued by the thought that my grandmother was named Zelda Zenderhoffer or something.

I finally realized that it might be time to consider letting go of the family actress grandmother story. That was harder to do than I thought it would be though because the actress-grandmother fantasy had been such a powerful presence in my childhood. It had become part of who I was. Giving it up was maybe being a little like those ghosts that don't realize they are dead.

In my heart, I think I was still holding out for Lucille Ball and Maureen O'Hara.

Naturally this gave the whole adopted mother's deathbed story with my mom declining to finally get the name of her biological actress mother, its' own death too. Like Luke Skywalker blowing up the death star.

It made me wonder about how the story even got started in the first place. Did it begin with a desperate little foundling girl trying to feel special? Making herself special with a movie star mom? I remember fantasizing as a child about being a famous cowgirl or astronaut. Was it something like that, something that just eventually took on a life of its' own? So much of a life that it really felt true and eventually *became* so true that it was the story that she even told her three little girls? The story that she eventually believed to be true in her heart. Her poor broken heart.

The actress grandmother story was untrue. I find myself wondering if the the story of the foundling hospital, dying baby and the nun's bizarre death request to the Grays, were untrue also. Did my mother want to, need to, believe it all – and be the most special one in all of the stories? Do moves like that come from deep feelings of inadequacy? Feeling unmoored? Feelings like a needy orphan might have who believed she was unwanted might have? Would these stories be crucial to keep her heart hole from cracking even more?

Of course they would.

My poor, poor mother. Why did she need to be part of something so big, so important? Why couldn't she just be a regular kid?

I think we all know the answer.

It's my hope and wish that my mother eventually found a way to accept the precious person she was. A precious, regular person. Nothing famous or spectacular, just a good person living a good life. Was that eventually enough for her? Was she able to finally find peace with herself? She wasn't one to ever talk about these things, so I don't really know. I sure do hope so though.

But now it's time for me to grow up and move on- as just a regular granddaughter of a regular grandmother.

Good bye Lucy. I'm going to so miss being your granddaughter. Thanks for being the stand in for so long at a time when we three really needed you. You have no idea how you sustained three little girls throughout their childhood.

I will still love you forever and for always!

15

HELEN THE LOST COUSIN WHISPERER

ANCESTRY.COM HAS A NICE FEATURE called Shared Matches. By clicking on it, the user can see everyone who's genetically connected to the person the user is trying to match. With one click, I could find everyone related to the Kellys or my paternal grandmother and grandfather.

I was assuming that anyone who showed up as a relative of mine but was not connected to those three branches of the family might be connected to my maternal grandmother. That's all the information I had on this elusive grandmother – a list of people she *wasn't* related to. Oh boy, not so much.

Helen came up as a third cousin to me. She was not connected to any other branches. Third cousin! That probably meant that our great-grandparents were siblings. That blew me away. I could also see the names of all the people who were connected to us both. People with the family name of Baxter seemed to be at the center of this group.

I was feeling more confident now and wasn't making as many crucial errors lately. I was getting better at this genealogy stuff. Third cousins? Aaaah, no problem. Piece of cake.

Or maybe humble pie?

Helen is one of the kindest, most welcoming people that I've met in this quest. And she only lived about an hour away.

I call her the Lost Cousin Whisperer because it seems to be her karma to guide the lost cousins. People wind up at her back door like feral cats looking for a bit of food and maybe a warm rug to nap on. As I write this, I'm thinking she's more like *Peter Pan* though, dealing with lost cousins instead of lost boys.

I had initially contacted her just before she was going to Florida for a month or so in the winter. She was sweet, but too busy to figure out who I was. I didn't try contacting her again for quite some time. After the terrorism allegations, I was more cautious, plus I was still busy figuring out all the Kelly stuff. I'd get back to it later.

In the summer of 2018, I was becoming disheartened. I wondered if I'd ever find my grandmother. I couldn't seem to find a path to her. Every day I'd check the new cousin list on Ancestry to see if a missing cousin or a desperately missed unknown sibling had tested. I was starting to feel like those anthropologists who have to move a gazillion buckets of dirt to see if they can find a tiny hominid finger bone fragment of a child who died thousands of years ago.

I had actually volunteered on an anthropology dig before starting grad school. It was a last, desperate attempt to make sure I didn't want to study anthropology. I almost immediately discovered that I didn't have the focus, attention or temperament to dig through dirt for eight hours a day. I was ready to jump off a cliff. On the other hand, the guy who was managing the dig looking for Native American artifacts was just adorable. But – oh dear – it turned out he had a girlfriend. That was the end of my archeology adventure.

I was starting to feel the same way about this quest as I did about digging for Native American artifacts. I wondered if my goal was even attainable. It seemed forever since I had found a good, new clue. I was losing the thrill of the search as I hit one dead end after another. And I was starting to accept that I might not be successful with finding my grandmother. It's something I always do – change my perspective to accommodate whatever the worst case scenario might be. I began thinking that Joe Kelly might need to be enough.

Then I remembered Helen.

I honestly don't know how I even forgot about her in the first place. I contacted her again, and fireworks went off for me. She was the cutest thing. It was like she hopped on a little rocket ship with me and agreed to blast off to the moon. She insisted I get on Facebook with all of her kids, cousins, siblings and other relatives so I could see the family and get a sense of who they are.

It was pretty shocking to me, but she seemed almost indifferent to finding out exactly how we were related. Just knowing we were cousins seemed enough for her. I didn't really understand her, but I will forever be grateful for her kindness.

Helen's cousin Jerry and her sister Ronnie sent me "Welcome to the family, cousin!" memes and emails. Their exuberance was a lovely sort of insanity to me. I am still in contact with them. I remained cautious about possible weird terrorist threats from these people who, in truth, were still strangers to me. It all seemed too good to be true. When I joked with Helen about half expecting the police to show up, she sent me a meme with police cars with sirens on. Bizarro humor too, hopefully that was a good sign.

Helen's family could look back on generations of relatives who all seemed to revere one another. They grew up feeling secure, loved and part of something bigger than themselves. They didn't seem suspicious or paranoid about me. They just seemed excited to have a new family member. They didn't appear as burdened by trauma? Many of them worked in the railroads too (that was another possible grandmother connection I was trying to sort through). I went back to the Jersey City railroad connection again, but couldn't find a Baxter – Kelly nexus. But the Baxter's weren't really laborers. They were conductors and engineers. There was probably more money and resources in this family. Maybe they weren't as burdened with the trauma of poverty. Maybe that's why they were so welcoming? I don't really know. But the mystery of how we were connected to each other sure seemed a little exciting for them?

Many of them sent me pictures, newspaper articles and stories of their family. My family. I was looking at the faces of my mother's family although I didn't know exactly how they were related to her.

But the "being raised by an orphan thing" seemed to kick in for me. I was feeling simultaneously stunned, thrilled, baffled and so very lucky as I basked in their warm, loving welcome. I must have done something pretty good in a prior life to deserve all this love from this good, good family. Lucky me!

I believed that Helen really was my best chance for finding my elusive grandmother. If she really was my third cousin, and if a set of our great-grandparents really were siblings, I was back in the game again.

The first thing I did was look at her great-grandparents. Every one of them seemed to have a half dozen siblings and children who, in turn, had a half dozen children. Oh my. This was going to be a big job. Helen didn't seem to know about too much more than her immediate family and grandparents. This meant I would need to do a backwards family tree on everyone and start ruling things out.

I was thrilled to have a focus again, though. This process is pretty interesting and oddly delicate. It was hard for me not to feel I was snooping around in other people's business. Even though the people I was looking at had all been dead for up to two hundred years, it still felt weird for me. I was trying to balance being respectful of the family privacy versus getting the information I needed to find my grandmother. I tried to avoid researching people who were born after my mother unless it was an obscure branch – so I could research possible hidden DNA links. I was trying to balance being respectful while still getting the information that I needed. The job became very big as I also had to research all of the people who married into the family and *their* siblings, aunts and uncles and grandparents, kids and so on. I needed to look at hundreds of people.

I realized pretty quickly that I had to develop a system of ruling women in or out.

As with the actresses, I felt that if women in this family were married and had young children, then they probably wouldn't have been having an affair with nineteen-year-old Joe Kelly. I felt it was also unlikely that they would have run into each other because teenage boys on the prowl like Joe, would probably not be hanging out in the same places as women with babies and toddlers. Recalling how unsexual I felt after having a baby and while parenting young children, it seemed unlikely they would have hooked up with him regardless of his many charms. Of course, there was always church. People meet one another at church. I don't know if Joe even attended church.

I also ruled out any young women who were not living near the Kellys or close to public transportation. When my mother was conceived in 1920, it was uncommon for families to have a car. I figured that I really needed to look at women who lived in his Manhattan neighborhood. I kept Jersey City in my search as a possibility as there were ferries going back and forth between Manhattan to Jersey City. Joe's cousins, including the other Joe Kelly, still lived there.

And I ruled out women who were on the older side of childbearing age. If they were married and had kids, so it was hard to see how they could be taken in by a teenaged boy.

This process knocked out a lot of contenders.

The part that bothered me, and still does though were the few people I couldn't pick up the trail on. I had their names but didn't know if they married or had kids. It was also possible that some of the men fathered a daughter and didn't even know it. Perhaps like Joe Kelly? There were many dead ends.

To complicate matters, it seemed that everyone in both families had common names. With so many people bearing the same names, it was sometimes pretty much impossible for me to tell who was who.

It was a daunting process and took months.

Helen eventually introduced me to her cousin Penny's husband,

Charlie. Charlie was the family historian and genealogist. And get this – they lived just one town away from me! Charlie sent me the coolest family pictures ever, and he even invited me to their house so we could compare notes and share information. Charlie and Penny were so lovely. They were living with their very Irish grandchildren and children. The wee ones were cherished and well cared for. Their house was stunning.

What a family I had bumbled into! I needed to buy a lottery ticket or something as my luck was running high.

Charlie is a much better researcher than I. He had a lot of tips for me, along with records and pictures to show me. He filled in some of the missing people on my family tree. And he urged me to get a family tree program for my computer that could accommodate the very large tree I was making.

The orphan thing kicked in after I left. Why were these strangers being so kind? Why were they opening up family information to a cousin who was little more than a stranger? Why did they seem so invested in helping me finish my quest?

I tried sorting out my befuddlement. Wouldn't I try to do the same for someone else? Isn't it a human default to be helpful? My brain was aching with all of these existential thoughts.

Charlie became a trusted comrade who taught me how to approach people. I sought his advice quite a few times, and he was always gracious and wise.

It was through this process and with Charlie's help that I came up with two main contenders for Grandma.

Rosina and Olga.

16

FOLLOWING THE EVIDENCE

BEFORE I GO FURTHER, I want to explain why I am not going to use a lot of last names and pictures here. Charlie explained that the family members prefer to keep their research anonymous. He has a lot of information he could post online, but he chooses not to. I agreed to respect their privacy and not make public any pictures or information that I didn't find independently. When we met, we didn't speak about a book because I hadn't started writing it. Ha! He later said I could use his first name. I am hoping this won't dilute any interest for the reader. The process will still be expounded upon as will the emotions.

Okay. Through Helen, Ronnie, Jerry and Charlie, I was on a magic carpet ride. I was so focused on my goal and research that I didn't really think about what it would feel like to actually find my grandmother and try to piece together what the heck happened.

As explained in the last chapter, I went through a gazillion names. In ruling out as many people as I could, I had to take this very large family and every person attached to it back to the mid-1800s. It was my goal to avoid missing an obscure branch of the family. That was insane to me. Before starting his process, I couldn't go back past my own mother. Now I was going back to the mid-1800s. This could not be my life.

I imagine it must be how the people who found the Lascaux Caves in France felt when they casually stepped inside thinking they were just in a regular cave and then realized they were standing in the exact place that our prehistoric ancestors communed with their gods, animal spirits and each other. How does one step into sacred spaces and not feel the cosmic residue of time, energy and their own heart beating just a little bit differently? Forever differently. I believe that every life is presented a few opportunities and moments of pure grace (if we're really lucky and blessed). The grace of our own humanity, both bumbling and mystical.

For me, seeing the movements of this family (the Baxters) and the Kellys for nearly a couple of hundred years was an unimaginable honor and privilege. It was an opportunity for grace that I hoped to appropriately cherish.

As was the case with the Kellys, the Baxters had little choice but to leave their countries, their families and their homes. Starvation, jaw breaking poverty and the human drive to save their children seem to be what provoked these desperate moves. Again, Ireland and England were prominent; mostly Ireland. It also seems that being widowed was a primary motivation. There were so many widows and widowers. How does one even keep going? Was it the strength of desperation? Or the parental instinct? I don't know. What I do know is that I have serious doubts that I could have done what they did. I honor their sacrifice and am thrilled their blood flows through me.

Here's a good example of what I'm talking about. It's the story
of Rosina; one of my main contenders for a grandmother. In
1900 Daniel Baxter married Gabriella Racek when he was just
twenty-two and she was a mere twenty-one years old. They
were in New York City just getting started. Shortly afterward,
her parents both died within two to three days of each other.
I have not gotten their death certificates but there was both
a flu epidemic in the city as well as a huge snowfall. Maybe
fire? Maybe froze to death? Accident? See? These become the
questions. One piece of research leads to another. Anyway, the
bride's parents were from Bohemia. The bride's sister's name
was Rosina. Rosina was born in 1890. And was an orphan by
age 14.

For a Christmas gift the previous year, Louis had gotten me an
MTDNA test (a maternal DNA test). Bohemia would be consistent with the MTDNA test results.

A word about the MTDNA test. The test looks at only the maternal line – the DNA that gets passed down from mothers to
daughters for hundreds of years. It is a direct genealogical line
to my grandmother's people. It was a spectacular gift, and one I
desperately needed.

I wound up having just one zero-degree match, Mark. A zero-
degree match means that there is a 50 percent likely possibility
that the connection between his maternal line and mine occurred
within five generations, about one hundred twenty-five to one
hundred fifty years ago. It sounds like a lot and it is, but lately
two hundred years ago no longer seems so much.

His family tree indicated that his (and my) maternal ancestors
were from the regions of Baden, Germany and Prussia. I had
to look up where Prussia really is/was. As the boundaries of

countries in that region of the world keep changing because of political, religious and historical influences, it's hard to pin it down exactly. Certainly Germany, part of France and Russia could be considered part of where Prussia is and was.

Learning that my grandmother came from that part of Europe was a complete shock to me. Why would I be shocked at anything? The story of the actress grandmother coming from Ireland somehow made Ireland stick in my brain as the only possibility of maternal origins. I imprinted on Ireland. See? See how our thinking gets stuck? We think that what we know is the only truth and can't always see other options right in front of us. Well, that's true for me at least.

Mark's earliest maternal ancestor Susanna Armbruster, appeared to be from Baden, Germany. I wound up doing an extended family tree on Susanna based on his family tree. I was looking for any intersection of names and locations. I believe this is called a backwards family tree, it's where you start from the past and work your way up to the present. The typical process is where we start with ourselves and work our way back to the past. When you're looking for old ancestral links, it often starts from the past, not the present.

Throughout this entire process, I created about ten to twelve family trees and researched and documented about 700 people from different branches, trying to find a connection between their families and mine. I was looking to find a nexus with my family. The 700 people didn't include the hundreds of people I determined were not relatives. This can be a grueling process. For example, every time I verified a census, I would look at the neighbors of the person to see if anyone from the different trees were neighbors. It's like a neural network with a gazillion pieces branching off in a gabillion directions.

Anyway, Rosina – the sibling of Daniel Baxter's bride, Gabriella – had an eleven-year-old brother. Rosina was fourteen years old when her parents died within a few days of each other. This young couple took them in! Does anyone reading this know of any young couple today who could support, not only themselves, but two children?

It is utterly amazing, yet consistent with the times. People just sucked it up and got the job done. I generally get lost in the "What if's."

Rosina was older than Joe Kelly. Given all of the trauma she had survived, though, she certainly could have been vulnerable to the attention of a handsome young man. She was a prime candidate.

Until she wasn't.

I followed her story and realized that she had married young and moved out of the country. Until then, she was the only possible candidate. I had gotten attached to her and her devastating story. I didn't really want to let Rosina go. That's odd right? I can't really explain it. Reading and piecing together the stories of these long dead people somehow created, for me, a sense of knowing them. In imagining how they felt and wondering at how they continued along, it made me feel awe at how tenacious their need to survive and thrive was. I think it's sort of the same process as to why people who survive the same trauma (like a plane crash) often wind up getting together. Or maybe it just might be residue from being raised by an orphan? Who knows?

But I still had one last possibility: Olga Crowe Martin. I reluctantly moved on from Rosina and took a closer look at Olga. Helen's great-grandfather Baxter had married a Martin. Emma Martin. I wound up starting another tree back from the two of them. I was clearly very related to all of their grand children. I was just starting to consider that it might not be the Baxter line that I was genetically connected to, but the Martin line. Remember, I had to research everyone who married in to the family and all of their genetic connections too.

I saw that Emma Martin Baxter had died early, at age forty-one in 1915. Louis and I went on another hot date to the Hall of Archives in New York City to find Emma's death certificate. It revealed that she had died under unusual circumstances and that there had been a coroner's inquest. The cause of death, though, was illegible. That was concerning. Inquests are done for murders, accidents, when someone finds a body etc. Basically when there's any sort of unusual death, it must be investigated to rule out foul play. What on earth had happened to poor Emma?

Since we were already where the records were, we were able to get a copy of the coroner's report, too, thanks to Barbara Hibbert, (one of the supervisors at the New York City Municipal Archives Reference room). Barbara was another one who always was willing to go the extra mile with me. I will always be grateful for her help. Anyway, we found out that Emma had dropped dead in a drug store from a fatal cardiac event. I found myself tearing up a bit. Who would want to die alone like that? In public? Without her loved ones with her? With strange people staring at her. Watching her die. Was she there trying to get some sort of tonic for her cardiac symptoms? Forty one is a very young age to die like that. But back then, dying from things that are no longer fatal today was common. Many died from simple infections. She left four young children, one of them became Helen's grandmother.

It was such a sad, sad thing for me to read. I felt I knew her. I was clearly related to all of her kids' kids. She was genetically

very, very close to me. Charlie showed me the only known picture of her. I honestly thought that she did kind of look like my
mother. Did she really? I was stunned when I looked at it though
and saw the resemblance. Was it wishful thinking? Desperation?
Not trusting myself, I sent the picture on to my sisters. They, too,
could see a strong resemblance but they also weren't sure. I felt
maybe I was on the right path.

What was crucial about getting the original document, though,
was that on her death certificate, her parents were listed as
Charles and Johanna Crowe. Crowe? I thought her name was
Martin. I did more research and rechecked the census records and
found them. I could find them all first as Crowes, then Johanna
was a Martin, while all the kids were Crowe Martins. Johanna's
first husband Charles had died. Johanna had remarried and her
new husband Robert Martin, had adopted the kids.

Adoption! That was a crucial piece of hidden information.

Everyone on Ancestry had my Emma confused with another
Emma Martin, who was also from New York State and about the
same age. So now my family tree consisted of two Joe Kellys, two
Emma Martins, two Delia Burkes and two Catherine Dowlings.
That's almost not cosmically fair for a novice genealogist to get
slammed like that, but there it was. Doing the math, checking
dates, places and double checking everything was so crucial.
These are the things that make novice genealogists get so en-
tangled in errors, myself included.

I then turned my attention to Emma's siblings and her husband's
siblings. Remember I learned from Helen's DNA that there was
a likelihood that our great-grandparents were siblings. Emma
was Helen and Ronnie's great-grandmother. Emma had older

siblings, but they seemed too old. The math wasn't right, even for their daughters, who would have been too young.

Then I looked at James Crowe Martin, Emma's younger brother. He had married Louise Koehler. Get this. Louise's maternal grandparents were from Baden, Germany!

That fit exactly into the MTDNA data.

I had one of my sons do a DNA test on My Heritage and was stunned that he showed no Irish in him. I was about 60 percent Irish, so how could he have none? He came up as primarily German, French and Russian. His father was Polish, which is close enough to the Slavic people. How could that even be? Did they switch babies at the hospital? Have I been loving someone else's child for more than two decades? Nah... our centimorgan count was crazy high. He's mine

Since then, I have come to realize that this is not really that uncommon. DNA is very fickle. Remember my sister always has twenty to thirty more cousins than I do and some of the cousins we have aren't related to each other or both of us. It was very hard for me to wrap my mind around it. Turns out, though, that DNA is never wrong.

Anyway, James and Louise had two children: Olga, who was two weeks older than Joe Kelly; and Ken, who was about four years younger than Olga. Could Olga be my grandmother? By then I had experienced enough disappointment to not allow myself too much hope.

Maddeningly, the 1920 census doesn't show James, Louise, Olga and Ken Martin anywhere. Nowhere! How could that be? They were in the Bronx in 1915 and in Jersey City in 1925 (according to data in the Jersey City directory).

1920 and 1921 were the crucial years. What the heck happened to them? They all seemed pretty free and easy, vacillating between the Crowe, Martin and Koehler names. I checked every combination I could think of. No luck. Were they trying to hide? Hide a pregnancy? Or did they just move and inadvertently miss the census takers?

In New York State, no one can get copies of birth records for people born after 1909. Is that crazy or what? The birth records after that time have now been private for one hundred and ten years. For what? For whom? Nonetheless, I looked for births with Olga Martin, Olga Crowe, Olga Koehler in late 1920 and early 1921. I couldn't find anything to bring it all home. It was maddening.

I found that Olga hadn't married until 1930, when she wed John Servante. They never had children. Why was that, I wondered. Was one of them barren? Who knew?

I couldn't prove anything. Was Olga my grandmother? She was the primary contender. If I am honest, she was the only contender.

Initially I became disheartened. I wasn't sure where to look next or what to even look for. All the paths to my grandmother seemed blocked. I felt that I had only one choice left to me.

I did what any serious genealogy researcher would have done next.

I made an appointment with a psychic.

17

CAN THE PSYCHIC REALLY BRING IT ALL HOME?

In September 2018, I was talking to a woman about her experiences with a medium. I have to admit that I always thought that, at best, mediums were a shaky sort of concept and, at worst, a potentially unkind, brutal thing to do to someone who is maybe in some sort of pain or distress. Kind of like having to swallow fish oil to possibly stop the onset of elbow cancer or something like that.

Anyway, she liked the medium, she said, "because she gave me a lot of names."

Names? Did she say a lot of names?

That's what I needed. A name. *The* name. The name of my elusive grandmother. I decided to call her medium, Stacia. I loved that name because it was a little exotic. I was shocked when she offered me an appointment for the very next day. I took it.

The nano-second I hung up I started wondering though why Stacia was so available. How come she had free time? Maybe she was a fraud? In the end, I decided it was irrelevant. It wasn't that much money. I could certainly afford to waste it. I told myself that I didn't really care, and it didn't really matter. I'd never gone to a psychic before and lived a happy life. What could it hurt?

The next day, as I headed over to her house I was shocked that I found myself with a little bud of hope that maybe she could help me get unstuck in my search. I felt like one of those turtles that keeps trying to cross the street and people keep picking him up and putting him closer to the wrong side, forcing the poor creature to start his journey across the road over again. And again and again.

Olga was the only contender for grandmother, but I didn't really have much on her. Certainly not enough to rule her in or out.

I started having a feeling that my reading with Stacia was maybe going to be a girl ghost visit thing. Was it a wish or a feeling? Who knew? Regardless I was feeling hope that maybe I'd catch a break.

Just having that little bit of hope was like being at a spa for me. I think the difficulty of this quest was starting to get to me a little bit. I didn't even realize that it impacting me like that. I didn't think it would be so hard for so long. Was I becoming too obsessive? Too focused on finishing the quest? Maybe being with Stacia would be like being at the beach watching dolphins play. A little psychic vacation

I pulled up to Stacia's neat beige house. Beige? What kind of psychic has a beige house? I think I was expecting (or hoping) that it would be purple with day glow alien green shutters, something like that. Beige? Good grief.

She came out and told me where to park. She, too, dressed a little beige, wearing non-descript pants and shirt. Was she wearing scrubs? Her hair was in a ponytail. No make-up. The type of woman anyone might walk right past in a grocery store. I have to admit, I had recently discovered The Long Island Medium TV show and appreciated Theresa Caputo's crazy hair, nails and clothing and presumed all mediums had a theatrical quality. Stacia didn't. I had expected someone exotic and a little wild. Stacia was very grounded and friendly and had a sweet charm about her. She was very pretty in an understated way.

I went inside. There were no doorway beads to push past. No incense. No crystal balls. No rose-colored light bulbs. Just a neat suburban family home with family pics on the wall. Geez.

She took me to an inside porch. Was it overlooking a pool? She grabbed a water bottle from a little fridge that she had on the porch. I noticed there was also beer in the fridge. She saw me looking at them and asked if I wanted one. I was mortified that she saw that. Do men feel like that when they get caught looking at a woman's boobs? I don't even drink beer. Now that I look back, I think I probably should have taken a cold one.

I had only given her my first name. I didn't want her looking me up and knowing anything about me. I didn't tell her anything about why I was there, partly because I wanted her reading to be pure, and partly because I was so uncomfortable that I was even there in the first place.

I started to ask her what I was supposed to do. Look away in case her head started spinning? Naturally, before I even got the question out, she explained her process. She said she just talks and shares what she sees and hears. Ummm, okay.

Before I could ask anything or process what she was saying, she told me that four women were stepping forward. Four! Wow. The first was Anne or Annie. Everyone in the world knows a dead Ann. Except me. Before I could respond she said, "Patricia." I didn't respond as I couldn't think of any deceased Patricias. There were quite a few Patricks Kellys, though. Is that what she meant? I didn't tell her that. I was trying hard not to react and give her hints. Besides, what did I really even know, anyway?

Then she mentioned Louise or Louisa. Hmmm. That was the name of Olga's mother. It was also Olga's middle name. Coincidence? Well okay; that was odd. Not a common name. Stacia had my attention. I found out later it was also the name of Olga's grandmother and great-grandmothers and a thousand aunts and cousins. Louise was the family name.

Then she said, "Barbara." Barbara? That's my mother's name! Certainly not a common name. She said that Barbara was saying that she wanted to help me but didn't know the answer. I could feel myself tearing up a bit. My mother had been dead for twenty-eight years and even the thought of her trying to communicate with me was so touching. Even if it was a stupid scam, it was sweet and moving. She asked if Barbara was connected to Trinity. I said no as I didn't know a Trinity. Then Stacia asked about a trinity of people. Three people? Then she said, "No no no. Three girls." I have two sisters. I nearly fell off the chair. Damn. Wow. And Oh My God!

Then Stacia was off to the races and asked about a seamstress. Someone who made clothes. And dancers? My father's maternal grandmother was a seamstress for the Ziegfeld Follies! I was annoyed that she showed up, though. My father, uncle and grandmother always talked about how unkind and mean she was. I wasn't really interested in her at that point and was a little resentful that she was taking up Stacia's precious time.

She asked about an attractive woman, well dressed with perfect make-up. I had no clue.

Then she asked about a Jean or Gina. She kept tapping her head and asking about an aneurysm or blow to the head. My uncle Donald's wife, Aunt Jean, had died of an aneurysm. I was stunned. She had been a precious person in my childhood.

Kathy or Katherine? My mother's middle name. Oh boy.

Then William? William is my father! I was pretty shocked that he came. He wasn't the type to put much stock in this stuff. Stacia said he was with a tightwad penny pincher who wouldn't open his purse. Something around a ball? Bowling maybe? My father was an avid golfer. I couldn't think of a tightwad golfing buddy. She said they had a regularly scheduled time around some sort of sport with a ball. It was as I was driving home later that I realized Stacia may have been referring to my paternal grandfather. After my paternal grandparents divorced, my grandfather visited my father once a year, bought him a suit and took him to a baseball game. Oh my God! Again!

I know this is all sounding unbelievable. But it really happened and in the order and way I am presenting it. I have to be honest, if I were reading this, I'd probably have my doubts. I still can't believe it myself.

Then she mentioned a Joe or Joseph. She said that he was there with three female friends or three girlfriends with him. Good grief! Joe Kelly? My grandfather? My mother's biological father? It sure sounded like him being with the three women. But I honestly just couldn't think about him then. This was about my grandmother this time; not him. I didn't react at all. I think I was somehow reluctant to go down the Joe Kelly path that day. It's funny, I had my own little agenda in my head and didn't want to divert from it. Like I can control ghostly visitors.

She then mentioned someone connected to an Anthony. An Italian. That was odd as no one would ever look at me and think there was any Italian in me. I am very fair skinned, blue eyes, sort of dirty blond – light brown hair. I blew it off. Boy, was that a big mistake.

She kept going back to the Italian man and said he kept showing her his dark arms. She said that he owned a restaurant. Half of me was thinking that my boyfriend Louis's family may have been trying to get a message to him. He's the guy with the Italian family, not me. None of them owned restaurants though.

Stacia mentioned a few times that someone in the family may have had business with watches. Jewelry? Gambling? It didn't resonate.

Until I got home ...

... and remembered that Olga had married an Italian man, John Servante, who had a restaurant. Not just a restaurant; but a *restaurant*. The Clam Broth House in Hoboken, New Jersey. It was a favorite haunt of Frank Sinatra and his mother, as they were also from Hoboken. Sinatra's movie star friends hung out at The Clam Broth House. President Hoover sent troops to war from the Clam Broth balcony. The movie *On the Waterfront* with Marlin Brando was filmed right in that area and the film crew spent time at the restaurant. There's even a line in that movie that may refer to The Clam Broth House: "Get your stinking clam breath away from me."

The building had been designated as an historical landmark, but it was taken down, before it fell down years ago. Everything is gone – all except for the original neon sign, which is still where it always was. It's a huge hand pointing the way to The Clam Broth house. Louis and I actually went there to check it out. There's a new restaurant on the same spot where the Clam Broth House was, it's called Biggies. They still make an homage to the history of the location and continue to serve clam chowder there. I had two bowls of amazing Manhattan clam chowder there. It was honestly the best chowder I've ever had.

The Clam Broth House sign that is still on the roof where the original sign was that pointed the way to The Clam Broth House in Hoboken, New Jersey. The sign is now a historical marker.

At home, I looked up Olga's husband's military records. He described himself as a dark-skinned Caucasian. Just like Stacia said!

There were rumors that maybe mob types hung around The Clam Broth House. Maybe that's where the gambling, jewelry and watches came in? John and Olga seemed to be on the wealthy side. In one census, it was reported that there was no source of income although the other census records show they were in the restaurant business. Mostly, though, they listed themselves as working in the restaurant business.

Now get this. John's parents were named Anthony and Antoinette. Damn, Stacia got it again.

Wouldn't it be insane if Joe Kelly had gone to The Clam Broth House? Both Joe and Olga seemed to be running with a famous crowd. There certainly could have been spill over. My mind was running wild, like an out of control freight train.

But I digress.

Back to Stacia. She had mentioned a bunch of things and names that didn't resonate: Bernadette, Christine, Kevin, Thomas, twins (I would come to find out that twins do run in both sides of my mother's family). I still don't know what to make of them all.

She talked about a young man, maybe in his early twenties, with blue eyes, dark hair and a mustache dying in some sort of freakish accident. He showed up a few times and seemed persistent and insistent that he make his presence known. Remember him- as there's more about him later.

And she insisted a woman named Maureen with a common last

name like White, Smith, Brown or Jones would be a crucial person, and that I should pay attention to that. Okay? Okay.

She also mentioned a Ken or Kenneth. Again, not a common name. I remember thinking, Who even knows a Ken? I forgot until I got home and checked on things. Olga's brother was named Ken. Oh my God yet again! Did my mother's uncle show up to help? Stacia was absolutely blowing me away.

Before we ended, she talked about twin sisters. Soul sisters? Sisters who were currently alive. One living near a beach. They would help introduce me to an older gentleman who knows the answers and would help me get pictures of my grandmother.

She saw a pastel portrait of my grandmother, too. OMG!

Could this be my sweetest new cousins through Ancestry – Helen and her sister Ronnie? Ronnie lives near the beach. They both have been the most welcoming people on the planet. They clearly treasure each other, the children and the elders. And even nutty cousins falling onto them from the sky.

Remember, they had introduced me to Charlie – the family genealogist and collector of photos, documents and cemetery records. He had sent me all sorts of pictures. He even had a pic of Olga's Aunt Emma. I was thrilled to look at the face of someone who knew Olga.

Could Charlie be the elderly gentleman the psychic talked about? He didn't really seem that old to me, but maybe he could have seemed old to Stacia? He had no pics of Olga.

I can't even say how he touched my heart, though. Who does that? I hope someday I can repay them all. Maybe bone marrow? Kidney? Something like that.

I know many people reading this (if anyone ever does), might think I'm a nut. I can't say that's not true, but everything I told you about Stacia is true. For real. I'm now a believer.

I left Stacia with renewed vigor. I would open up a more thorough investigation into Olga. The circle was tightening. Or was that my own brain starting to crack up? Or my own heart hole starting to close?

Maybe a little of both.

18

LIFE AFTER THE PSYCHIC ... OH BOY

WHEN I TOLD LOUIS I was going to a medium, he texted back three words to me: Research Research Research!

He's not a psychic kind of guy, and it was clear that he thought I was going way off course. He didn't use the word "ridiculous," but I am sure that's pretty much what he was thinking. But as he's a kind and supportive man, he didn't push it too hard.

I drove away from Stacia's with my head spinning and feeling combustible. I couldn't wait to talk to Louis. I made it about three blocks before I pulled over near a vacant lot that looked like a place to dump a dead body. I didn't care.

I told Louis everything. I didn't contact my sisters because they didn't seem as interested or as invested in this quest as he was. They said they found this research confusing and overwhelming. Besides, I wasn't sure how they felt about mediums.

I imagine that I might have sounded like one of those old re-cord players stuck and repeating the same thing over and over. I kept replaying in my head all that she said. Even Louis, the straight arrow, conservative guy, was stunned. There were a lot of "Wows, I can't believe that," and "Oh my God's" (much to his chagrin I am sure).

Both of us decided we needed to dig deeper on Olga. And try harder. The medium gave us the shot of enthusiasm that we desperately needed. Stacia was like 90 percent caffeinated dark chocolate for us.

Olga Crowe Martin, here we come!

I dug deeper and found her communion and confirmation records in the Bronx. Interestingly, her name was listed as Olga Louise Crowe Martin. There's the Crowe name again. It was touching for me in that it seems as if James continued to honor his biologi-cal father, Charles Crowe. James's father had been a blacksmith who died when James was only three. He left four other kids, too, one just a newborn or maybe even unborn. Would James have even had a conscious memory of his father? Or was it more of a heart hole thing? Charles was only about thirty-eight years old at the time of his death. A very young man.

It was difficult to read the cause of death on Charles Crowe's death certificate that Louis found. It looked initially like he might have died from delirium due to malaria.

Malaria? Who dies of malaria in New York City?

Come to find out, malaria has a long history in Europe and prob-ably came to this continent with Columbus, but it didn't really take hold until slaves were forced from Africa to the Americas.

The process of clearing land for housing and cities created a perfect environment for mosquitos to swarm. Malaria was a huge problem during the Revolutionary War and, by 1850, it was in every settlement on the East coast and most of the rest of the country.

Charles was a young blacksmith, so presumably he was strong. Who would expect that such a strong, young man would die from such a small insect? He survived the hard trip from Ireland as just a young teenager and gets taken down by a mosquito in this Promised Land? Geez.

Upon further study, though, we realized that Charles hadn't died of malaria but of Mania A Patu, otherwise known as madness from drinking alcohol or, the delirium tremens.

Charles drank himself to death.

Apparently, it took him two days to die from it as it was so bad. What a horror. What a waste of a life time of dreams and hope.

And what a trauma his death had to be for James' mother Johanna, now a young widow with five children (or maybe 4 with one on the way). Five very young children. Initially, I found myself becoming upset with Charles for dying in such a stupid, needless way. It was Louis who helped me be more compassionate. Being a blacksmith was a hard, rough life. His thirty-eight-year-old body had to be racked with pain. There was no Tylenol then. Just pain and no relief. How could anyone go on like that? Plus being burdened with the responsibility of five kids and a wife. Good grief. Alcohol made sense.

No wonder Johanna remarried so quickly after his death. What choice did she really have? She married Robert Martin. What a good man he sounds like, marrying a young widow with five very young children. Wow. Johanna blessed him with a daughter of his own pretty quickly.

Just an aside here: Robert himself was born at sea on his way to America from Europe. I found that to be pretty cool. Apparently, anyone born at sea takes the citizenship of whatever country the ship is registered to. That's interesting isn't it?

James was raised without one of his biological parents. He wasn't an orphan, but he seemed to deeply miss his biological father, as evidenced by how he kept the name alive in his children and himself. Did he know how Charles died? Did he have a reverence for those who came before? Keeping the Crowe name alive in his kids and continuing to use James Crowe Martin himself for his entire life was perhaps a response to a missing parent? Was it an orphan thing? A heart hole thing?

Charles Crow seemed to have worked in a carriage house making and repairing the carriage wheels. Interestingly, Robert Martin (whom Johanna later married) worked in a similar place, perhaps even the same place. And to add even more intrigue, Michael Kelly (Joe Kelly's father) was also a carriage driver. They all lived in the same area. Did they all work together? Did they know each other? Wouldn't that be wild? Could Olga Martin and Joe Kelly have met through their parents?

Placing whomever my grandmother turned out to be in the vicinity of Joe Kelly, has all along been my most complex and elusive challenge. Before I could really speculate about anything, I would have to have a reasonable explanation about how they could have met. That's not an easy thing to do for something that happened in 1920. I was hoping the genealogy fairies would drop a photo of the two of them together in my flower patch and close the deal. They never did.

Anyway, back to Olga. If the Crowe, Martin, Koehlers were trying to hide themselves or hide a pregnancy, maybe they would use different names. I looked through hundreds of census records, birth records, and so on, using every possible name combination. I didn't find them.

But Louis did!

He was looking at the New York City directories. The directories looked insanely boring to me, and I didn't pay much attention to them then. The directories came out about every year or two. The data was collected the year before they were published. Louis tends to be more methodical than I am. James Martin was not an uncommon name, so there were a ton of them to sort out and follow. Focusing on that level of detail has never been my strength. I am a painter and tend toward big, bold paint strokes that convey moods and feelings rather than specific detailed paintings. It's a good thing I didn't turn out to be a brain surgeon.

While Louis was meticulously cross referencing names, locations and vocations, he hit pay dirt.

He found the Martins living on the exact same block at the exact same time as Joe Kelly's family!!!

That brought it all home. That was it!

I felt a little like what I believe cancer survivors might feel when told they're in remission. It's what they hope for and work toward, but do they ever really expect the happy ending? I was stunned.

Olga and Joe were literally just around the corner from each other for at least two or three years. Just yards apart! The Martins were there in 1918 and 1919. The directories were researched and assembled in the previous year, which means the Martins were likely there from as early as 1917 through part of 1920. Joe and Olga may have even gone to school together.

Joe Kelly and Olga Martin were literally living around the corner from each other. They were the same age. When I heard that and realized the implication of this unbelievable news, I literally started feeling buzzy. Seriously buzzy.

A couple of years before this discovery, I had fallen off a ladder and broke my foot in three places. I knew it was bad, yet I did not feel pain. I was in severe shock and feeling dissociative and buzzy. Really buzzy. It was great until the shock wore off.

When I realized Joe and Olga lived around the corner from each other and maybe even went to school together, I was again in absolute shock. And buzzy. Happily buzzy this time. I didn't need painkillers for this one.

For the next week or so, every time Louis and I talked, the conversation became pretty much like, "Can you believe this? I just can't believe it! I just can't believe this!" And we really couldn't believe it. We had been searching so long and so diligently, that I don't think that either of us really thought about what the ending might look like. We were in complete shock.

But I had been mistaken so many times before that I couldn't really trust the idea that Olga may have been my mother's mother. We still didn't have proof. And, boy, was that going to be hard to get without a birth certificate. Remember the stupid law in New York state about not being allowed to get birth certificates for anyone born after 1909? That was going to be a mother of a problem. Get it? A mother of a problem?

I considered going to court to have myself declared, post mortem, as my mother's executrix, but that would have been a hard, desperate sell as she had been dead for twenty eight years. I probably couldn't have justified a reasonable need.

We were thinking of other ways to build a case. Again, I went back to ancestry.com. They have a search tool that allows us to look up any surname and see any DNA matches associated with that name.

I first put in 'Crowe.' The page lit up like the Christmas tree in Rockefeller Center. There were dozens and dozens and dozens of hits. That was encouraging.

I then put in Olga's mother's maiden name: 'Koehler.' Again, it was Christmas. A buzzy Christmas. Ho Ho Ho to me. Who else but Olga married those two family trees together?

Remember the MTDNA test that Louis had gotten me for Christmas? The one that traces back only the maternal lineage? My only match with the 0-degree distance had a maternal ancestor, Suzanna Armbruster from Baden, Germany.

I went back to Ancestry.com to use another feature that allows the user to look up specific places to see if there are any other relatives from an exact area. I put in Baden, Germany. Again, the screen lit up like Christmas. It was Christmas for me. Rudolph was coming.

It gets even better. I did a family tree and found that Suzanna Armbruster had married Jacob Clouse and had emigrated to the United States. Specifically, to Sullivan County, New York. *She just lived in the next town over from the Grays, about five to seven miles away.* More hugely supportive circumstantial evidence. That completely blew me away. What are the odds of that? I wish

I knew a statistician; I'm sure they'd tell me it was something like a 6.5 billion to one.

The circumstantial evidence was starting to become overwhelming that Olga Crowe Martin was, indeed, my grandmother. But that is still not conclusive proof.

Louis again came to the rescue and found Olga's niece Joan Lamont (Olga's brother Ken's daughter) who was in her late eighties but was still alive and married. Maybe my mother's first cousin. He even found a phone number. I just love the internet sometimes, the information we can so easily get is both wonderful but sometimes horrifying. This possible cousin of my mother was likely the only person alive who may have known that Olga had a baby as a teenager.

But Joan was seriously unwell.

I spoke with her husband Alton. From what I learned about them, they have a true love story. The real deal, even after decades together. Alton said that Joan was the only woman he ever loved, or ever would love. That was such a lovely thing for me to come to understand. It was like being sprinkled with fairy dust. I have no clue why I was so touched by that knowledge, but I was. It was comforting to think that someone in my mother's immediate family had found true love and happiness. Maybe as a counter balance to her adoption angst? I don't really know. Or maybe it was just comforting for me to know that true love exists and is real.

Anyway, Alton was eighty-nine years old. And he told me they had known Olga and her husband John! That blew me away like a tornado. In fact, Alton said he had recently thrown out about a thousand old pictures. When I heard that, I sincerely thought I was going to throw up. It was an involuntary response. Apparently, they were trying to get the house cleaned out.

Oh, good grief.

Joan was too sick to talk, but Alton was chatty and sweet. I didn't tell him that I thought that Olga may have been my grand-mother. I had learned that people often don't want their family story changed. They don't always want new relatives. Or maybe they just don't want to think badly about a loved one. Charlie and Louis had both advised me to go slowly. I did tell Alton that there were a few of us looking to fill in the family tree and that I was somehow connected to his wife through her father.

Alton told me about how their children had gifted them a bound family history book. What a great present, right? He began tell-ing me about the Martin/Koehler family history. I didn't learn anything new but was thrilled he was giving me time. He even invited me to come and see the book. How lovely is that? He prom-ised he wouldn't throw out any more pictures. He even agreed to send me some pictures of Olga and John if he found any. He asked if I could call back in a week or so.

It was one of the longest weeks of my life. In the meantime, I sent them a *Feel Better* card with a note and a couple of fancy choco-late bars. Chocolate always helps me feel better. I was hoping it was a family trait.

I called about a week and a half later. Alton seemed more stressed and tired. He said his wife now had a nurse in their home. It didn't sound like she was doing well. He was more abrupt this time and had to get back to her. My heart broke for him. I can't even imagine what it is like to be with someone forever and have them be so sick.

I backed off completely out of respect for their privacy, their struggle, and just plain courtesy. I just didn't think it was the right time to spring my Olga story on him. He clearly had more important things to tend to.

A few weeks later, I decided to send them one last letter, gently explaining that I thought Olga Crowe Martin might be my grandmother. I felt it was a Hail Mary pass; my last hope. I said that, if true, it must have been devastating for Olga and the family to have to deal with an out-of-wedlock teenaged mother situation. These were strict, moral times and Olga, the family and the baby would have all been ostracized and shamed. There really wasn't much choice besides adoption.

I was trying to soften the blow and leave a way to save face for Olga and the family. I offered to answer any questions they might have but didn't get too much into the DNA numbers. Alton was a retired physician and would certainly understand it all, but they had enough to manage.

Louis was upset that I had told them this would be my last letter. He felt I didn't need to close that door.

The very next day, I got a huge package from them! Our mail had crossed paths in the post office. The envelope was full of amazing genealogical research and old letters from one of their cousins. I must have made an odd noise when I saw it because my twenty-four-year-old son ran in asking if I was okay. It maybe sounded like I was having a heart attack. Maybe I really *was* having a heart attack.

Alton and Joan weren't breaking up with me! They were just pretty busy taking care of each other. They were octogenarians. Why would I think they would or could answer immediately? I was like a kid impatient with Santa's elves taking too much time harnessing up the reindeer.

The package was not about Ken's father, James Crowe Martin, but about Ken's wife's family. She was not related to me, but I was so very touched by the effort they had made. Again, more angels helping me on this search. Am I one of the most blessed people on the planet or what?

Alton had asked that I return all of the family research. I copied it all the next day and sent it back immediately. I wanted to be respectful and stay in their good graces.

I soon got another letter from them. The envelope was old and yellowed and was an odd, out-of-date size. Small. I opened it up and saw that there was a yellowed matching piece of paper with a note inside. When I pulled the note out, three pictures cascaded out of the envelope in the way that sparkles and glitter flicker from gluey preschool fingers making a treasure.

I was finally looking at Olga's face!

Olga Louise Crowe Martin, the author's grandmother, circa 1934
Photo courtesy of Alton and Joan LaMont

I keep talking about soul rocking moments in this book, but this was one of the biggest for me. For real. I was certain I was staring at the face of my mother's mother. The enigma. The mystery. The unknown one. Here she was. It was like finding Amelia Earhart. The Holy Grail. The impossible thing. I sure got happily buzzy again.

The picture of Olga showed her as one of a group of people in Joan's family. In fact, Olga was right up front with her arm around Joan, and Joan's little arm was around her. I immediately saw a resemblance to my mother. Different, sure, but a resemblance.

There's a childhood picture of my sister Dawn that looks exactly like a childhood picture of my mother (with her Amelia Earhart haircut). My mother and sister look almost identical to one of my mother's Kelly half sibling's childhood pictures. My mother was a blend of Crowe and Kelly for sure.

Louis was also excited to see the pictures. He studied them like a biologist watching cells divide through a microscope. He saw a profound sadness in Olga's face. Here she was with her arms around a child whom she clearly loved and who clearly loved her, yet she also looked forlorn. Was she thinking about the child she gave away? The picture was taken in 1934 when Olga would have been thirty-three years old and married to John Servante. She had no children of her own. Was my mother the only opportunity she ever had to have a baby? Did she know she'd never have another?

Or did she just get stung by a bee or something, and her expression was really a grimace, not sadness?

Her story is like a Shakespearian tragedy. I know my mother was always yearning for her mother. How could Olga not have been yearning for her only child?

I couldn't wait to call Alton and thank him. All I could say when he answered the phone was, "Oh Alton ..." I heard a pleased little laugh at the other end of the line. He was clearly happy at how deeply he had touched my life. He gave me one of the greatest gifts I've ever gotten, and I will be grateful to them both until the day I die. Even after.

Then I remembered Stacia, the psychic's prediction that an elderly man would give me a picture of my grandmother. Damn. She really nailed it again. I would consider an eighty-nine-year-old an elderly gentleman.

There was another picture of Olga in the yellowed envelope, too. It had been taken in 1936, just two years later. She looked bloated and unwell and at least a decade older than in the 1934 picture.

What had happened to her? I am not sure I will ever know.

Alton said he'd look for more pictures and send them my way if he found any more. That would be amazing. I'd love it if they find a childhood picture of Olga. It would be fun to compare it to my mother's childhood pictures and those of my sisters.

I was totally satisfied though with having looked upon the face of my grandmother. Satisfied and thrilled. I never really let myself hope for or expect another.

And then... Alton and Joan sent another one. Wow. This one was of Olga at age 54, at Joan and Alton's wedding. She looked healthier and wealthier. I was happy to see her face without the sadness of the earlier picture.

Perhaps she found her peace?

I sure hope so.

Left to right: Olga Martin Servante with Alton and Joan
Lamont at their wedding in 1955. Olga was 54 years old.

Photo courtesy of Alton and Joan Lamont

19

OLGA: THE GERMAN PAST SHAPED THE INTERACTIONS WITH JOE

I STILL DON'T KNOW WHETHER Olga is my grandmother with 100 percent certainty because I can't get the birth certificate. And believe me, it's just killing me. But in my heart of hearts, I'm pretty certain. Maybe someday someone close in that family will take a DNA test, and I will know for sure. Maybe the birth records will be released by the powers that be in New York state. Maybe Maybe Maybe. There's nothing more I can do though, and I am accepting that reality. I think it kills Louis even more than me though.

Meanwhile, I find myself thinking about Olga. My heart breaks for the trauma she must have endured. In 1920, getting pregnant while an unmarried nineteen-year-old had to be a social, familial and religious horror. Today it's not a big deal as about 46 percent of all babies born in this country are now currently born to single women. It's odd to think about what a non issue it is today and how catastrophic it was in 1921. In those days an illegitimate birth could absolutely ruin a family. Back in the day it was a devastating shame, primarily for the girl.

And she was just a girl; only nineteen. Poor, poor Olga.

The New York City directory indicates that the Martins moved back to upper Manhattan (near Lincoln Center) from the Hell's Kitchen area sometime in 1920. Was it an abrupt move? Was it to save face for Olga and the family?

My grandmother would have conceived my mother in May or June of 1920. Joe Kelly wound up enlisting about three to four months after my mother's conception. Oh boy.

It was not unheard of for the family of a poor pregnant girl to threaten the boy or his family. Maybe try to force a marriage, maybe just give him a good beating. By the time my mother was conceived, Joe's father, Michael Kelly, was dying of stomach cancer. I presume Michael was becoming weaker at that point and not able to do much to help his son. Besides maybe Olga's grandfather Charles Crowe and Michael Kelly were friends who may have even worked together at the carriage house? Charles as a blacksmith and Michael as a carriage driver? Maybe?

Maybe Joe never knew that he had impregnated this girl. Or maybe he tried to stay with her. Maybe he tried to be supportive and loyal. Or maybe not. Maybe he had moved on to another woman or was living an even faster life. These questions will likely never be answered. In many ways, I suspect it was a blessing that they didn't stay together.

What is true, though, is that it would have been nearly impossible for the Martins or Olga to keep the baby. An illegitimate baby was a shame that would have plagued them until their dying days. The shame would also have been an issue for the child.

My mother would likely have grown up shunned and ostracized if she had remained with her biological family. It's difficult to imagine Olga ever being able to find a good man to marry her and help care for her illegitimate daughter. Who would have wanted Olga in that very strict society with clear (yet impractical) rules of morality? Rules that she had clearly broken. It is unlikely that there would have been other men for Olga if she had kept the baby.

One man was devastating enough.

If Joe Kelly hadn't agreed to marry her, there was no choice but to have another family raise the baby.

I am reminded about Olga's mother Louise's harsh words to Jennie Gray. "Don't ever try to get in touch with the family again. No one except me knows about this baby." Did that warning extend to Olga? Those were the days when newborn babies were whisked away from their mothers immediately after birth. Did Louise tell Olga the baby had died? Did Olga believe her baby was dead? How would one even live with that level of manipulation and deception? It's just such an odd way to say something, that it feels like it might actually be true.

I personally believe that Louise kept or destroyed my mother's birth certificate. It's just speculation, but to me it's what makes the most sense.

Did Louise keep the birth certificate so the Grays could never return the baby? Never prove that the baby was really a Crowe Martin? Was Louise angry at the baby for maybe almost killing her daughter, Olga? Did the birth somehow leave Olga sterile? I was viewing Louise as the villain in this story for being so rough and heartless with sweet Jennie Gray. But maybe it was really Louise's way of loving and protecting her own daughter, even from her own newborn baby granddaughter.

We all do the best we can, I guess.

It had to be painful for both families, one worrying that the baby would be taken away, and the other worrying that the baby would be returned.

According to my Uncle Donald's letters, Jennie, too, was apparently a big keeper of secrets. Between the biological grandmother and the adoptive mother, the secret of my mother's birth was certainly safe forever.

Almost ...

Interestingly, Louise herself also grew up without a father, just like her husband James. For both James and Louise, their fathers had died young and unexpectedly, leaving toddlers and newborns. Was that the initial bond and attraction to each other for James Crowe Martin and Louise Koehler Martin? Were they trying to fill each other's heart holes with another person who knew exactly how they felt? Did they both feel a little orphany, too?

Louise Koehler Martin, the author's maternal great-grandmother, circa 1934
Photo courtesy Joan and Alton Lamont

Not so shockingly, I guess, Louise and her own mother both have a similar story as my mother did. Children without parents are sadly an intergenerational reality in this family. We got Louise's parents' names by ordering Louise and James's marriage certificate. A mother's maiden name has to be recorded on a marriage certificate. Louise's said her mother's maiden name was Louise Keppler and her father was Frederick Jr. Koehler. Another Louise.

Frederick died at age twenty-three, only a month after baby Louise was born. How sad is that? I have to admit that I wondered if Frederick was the blue eyed, dark haired young man with a mustache in his early twenties who died in some sort of tragic accident that the psychic had spoken about. He honestly sounds like he looked like how my son Zack now looks.

Frederick Koehler's death record says he died from "congestion of the brain" in October 1868. That is a catch-all diagnosis that is not used today. It might have been a brain bleed from a head trauma. Or maybe a subdural hematoma. or a blow to the head from a fall. Was his absence and the aftermath of his death what made his daughter, Louise Koehler Martin, so harsh and rough?

I also obtained the marriage information on Louise Keppler and Frederick Koehler (Louise Koehler Martin's parents). Louise Keppler was only seventeen years old when they married – and seemed to be a little pregnant, unless the math on the records is wrong. The same pregnancy dilemma that would happen to her future granddaughter, Olga. Isn't that just a fascinating family pattern?

*Just a note here about all of the Louise's in this part of the family. I am so sorry! Remember the psychic asking if there was a Louise in the family? Heck yeah there's a Louise, or three or four.

I totally appreciate how confusing it is to keep them all straight, it is for me too. I did my best to differentiate them all by using both their maiden and married names. I feel like it makes the writing clunky, but hopefully that will be mediated with clarity.

Interestingly, Louise Koehler Martin sort of lost her mother, too – just not from death. After Frederick's untimely brain death, Louise Keppler Koehler left Newark, New Jersey, and moved to an apartment in New York City next door to her parents and some of her siblings. Alone. Without her kids. Without her toddler, Frederick III or infant Louise Koehler (Martin). Why?

Louise Keppler Koehler's parents were apparently wealthy and had successful saloons and boarding house/hotel businesses in both New York City and Newark, New Jersey. The Koehlers and Kepplers likely had business interactions. In 1869, there was a Koehler Hotel in Newark that had formerly been called The Keppler Hotel. That was a year after Frederick's death. Baby Louise Koehler (Martin) and her brother Frederick were raised by their paternal grandparents in Newark. Is that how the Koehler's got the Keppler hotel? Was the exchange of the hotel some sort of child support payment for the Koehler's for raising their two young grandchildren? Who can say? Census reports label it as a boarding house. Advertisements label it as a Hotel. Naturally the Koehler grandmother who raised Louise Koehler (Martin) was of course also named Louise. Geez Louise!

Did young Louise Keppler Koehler have some sort of breakdown after her husband died so young and unexpectedly? Was it a postpartum issue? Her parents and siblings were literally a door away in the next apartment in New York. They could have helped. Or was Louise Keppler Koehler just not able to care for her kids then?

The Koehler grandmother, Louise, was sixty-two years older than young Louise Koehler (Martin). The Koehler grandfather, was sixty years older than young Louise and died before she was a teenager. All of this would have been a pretty rough start for anyone. Trauma, grief and loss.

It's easy to see how the loss of her parents and grandparents could have affected Louise Koehler Martin's development. Her soul, even. Did it contribute to Louise's decision to have someone else raise her own illegitimate granddaughter, my mother? It was the same exact process that sort of happened to her too. Did she maybe feel that it wasn't such a bad thing because she went through it and she felt she was fine? Was she fine?

We didn't find Louise Kohler Martin's mother again until her mother remarried in 1880. That was about 12 years after Louise's father died at age twenty-three. Again we had to get a copy of the marriage license to check we had the right woman. We did. Louise's mom, Louise Keppler Koehler married Thomas Lenehan and had 7 more children. Including a set of twins. Remember the psychic mentioning the twin thing?

Louise is back finally, finally with her mother when she was in her early 20's. That made me feel good to know that at some point my great grandmother got to be back with her mom, even if it was when she was an adult.

Again, more childhood loss and trauma. More heart holes. Again. Always again.

Frederick Koehler Jr.'s parents had emigrated from Germany to America in the late 1820s, and the Kepplers arrived in the 1830s. Why? Like the Kellys, they left their families, their friends and their countries. What would make families sacrifice so much?

One possible answer: War.

The Napoleonic Wars occurred in the early 1800s. Napoleon was finally defeated at Waterloo in 1815, but not before inflicting devastating chaos, war crimes and trauma on the general population. And it was happening all around the area where the Keppler's and Koehler's were from in Germany.

Around the time of Napoleon's defeat, the Congress of Vienna established the German Confederation of thirty-nine independent German-speaking states to coordinate them into one entity rather than separate economies. It's how Germany started to become the Germany we know today.

It was certainly a time of great turmoil; a hopeful yet dangerous time. It would take decades to rebuild and stabilize. It probably was not the safest place for a family, and not everyone was happy with what was happening. There was violence.

America was safer and offered more opportunity. I doubt anyone expected, though, that it would provide an opportunity to inflict yet more trauma on yet more parentless kids. The family did quite well economically and seemed very bright. German ingenuity.

By 1925, Olga and the family were living in Jersey City. Louise Koehler's family (the Koehler grandmother) were from Newark, just the next town over. There were a lot of Koehlers from Baden, Germany, living in Jersey City. Remember Baden, Germany, is where Susanna Armbruster is from.

Why did the Martins leave New York City? So Olga and the family could get a do-over after my mother was given away? New place, new beginning? To be closer to family? To get away from Joe Kelly? Unanswerable.

Both Olga and Louise seem to have been very bright. Both worked as administrators in a bank. That seems unusual – two women getting so far in a man's world at that time. I'd like to believe that if Olga felt she had to give her baby away, that she became wiser and stronger as a result of that experience. I hope she got strength from her second chance and never let her feelings for a man interfere with her life again.

I think that may be true.

Olga didn't marry until she was thirty years old – almost a decade after giving birth to my mother. That also was very unusual for the time. Thirty years old was spinster territory. Seems like she wasn't going to fall victim to a pretty face again. Good for her.

She married John Servante, who was fourteen years older than she was. They never had children. Why? Were there miscarriages? Maybe she got torn up during the birth with my mother and wound up having a hysterectomy? Or did Olga not have children ever again as some sort of self-imposed attempt at religious redemption? Or was it heavenly retribution for her sins? Was one of them infertile? This was a family of churchgoers, but they shifted between the Lutheran, Episcopal and Catholic religions. Good religious girls didn't get pregnant before marriage.

I would assume that knowing she had a child out there and not being able to raise her had to be devastating, and all the worse as she never had another living child.

Was it tormenting for poor Olga? It would have been for anyone I would think. It is such a tragedy that a choice she made at nineteen could have haunted her until she died at the age of eighty-seven.

I did a little research on The Clam Broth House in Hoboken, the restaurant John Servante owned when he married Olga. I've talked to a couple of Hoboken historians about the place and did an internet search. Interestingly, prohibition seemed to be a background character in the vital parts of Olga's life. Prohibition started in 1920 (the year my mother was conceived) and ended in 1933, just after she married.

The Clam Broth House had three entrances from the street, and there was a bar at each entrance. During prohibition, when the feds arrived to shut down one bar, people just shifted to one of the other two bars in the place. Sort of like a shell game. That sounds so wild and cavalier. It's interesting that the Kepplers also had saloon businesses not far from The Clam Broth House. Is that how the families met? Because they were in the same trade?

The Clam Broth House always made a cup of hot clam broth and crackers available to folks who needed to warm up or who were poor and hungry. The waterfront is a cold and brutal place. That was a sweet thing to do, feed the poor and hungry, give back, make the world a little kinder. I wondered whose idea that was. Olga's? John's? John's father, Anthony?

The Clam Broth House was one of the last two places in the New York City metropolitan area that denied women permission to enter the bar. That wasn't such a sweet thing to learn. That was in the 1970s. Olga was in her 70s and a widow by then. It is unlikely she had anything to do with the business at that point. That's a comforting thought. It's painful to consider that this resilient, smart woman was not treated with the respect she deserved.

Besides celebrities like Sinatra and Brando, presidents and musical artists, there have been rumors that some mob types hung out at The Clam Broth House, too.

Goodness. Little Olga Martin was certainly running with a fast crowd.

So was Joe Kelly.

Through Adolf Zuker and his association with Paramount Pictures, Joe was also running with movie stars, celebrities, presidents and military types. A couple of relatives told me he went off on secret missions for the CIA or perhaps it was the White House. Supposedly, he and his first wife went to a banquet at the Roosevelt White House. I was not able to verify any of that.

(By the way, as a complete aside, one of the relatives answered a burning question that has gnawed at me for decades. Did aliens really land in Roswell, New Mexico? According to the relative, Joe confirmed that yes, aliens really did crash in New Mexico. Ha! You didn't expect to get proof of that from this book, did you? Well, it's apparently the truth. No more wondering.)

As Olga and Joe were only a state line apart and were both in the New York City metropolitan area and were both running with the same famous crowd of singers, actors, presidents, politicians and maybe were near mobsters, one has to wonder if they ever ran into each other again after the baby was born. What would that have been like? Did she smash him over the head with a bottle of prohibited whiskey? Or did they talk it out? Some things are not meant to be known, I guess.

From what little I heard about Olga and John, they were wealthy people. Her niece's husband told me that Olga had expensive paintings that went to a museum after her death. I asked him if there was a pastel portrait of Olga (something the medium had mentioned). He said he didn't recall one. Bummer.

It's interesting that Olga and John lived in a ritzy section of Bergen County, New Jersey, toward the end of their lives. My mother used to take us shopping there sometimes. It was only about thirty-five miles away from where we lived. Certainly, we went there every Christmas because the real Santa hung out at Bambergers Department store to meet every child in the entire world there.

My mother used to love those colored glass balls on macramé strings that hung on a hook. They were sort of nautical looking. I don't know what they are called. We always went to Bergen county to a special store to get more when hers broke. (Actually, when my sisters or I accidentally broke them.) Is it possible that we were ever in the same store when Olga was there? Maybe Olga liked those nautical glass balls, too? Maybe we saw her? Maybe she saw three little girls running around and thought there was something oddly familiar about them? Or did the woman with the kids remind her of someone?

Or would she have thought we were a little too mismatched with second-hand clothes that didn't quite fit right? Alton told me that Olga was a sharp dresser. We were pretty poor. My parents made sure there was enough food, but we didn't have fancy new clothes or expensive things. I didn't get to pick out my first dress until I was in fifth grade. What a thrill. I picked out a snazzy little brown dress with cream lace. I can still picture it as I was so excited to finally have something that I chose for myself. I share this as a way to contrast how I feel that our lives were in sharp contrast to what I believe Olga's life was like. My mother was a simple dresser who never wore makeup – other than maybe a little lipstick sometimes, but that was about it. She was not stylish by any means.

But she was a brilliant, kind-hearted woman who loved her friends and family. We grew up absolutely knowing that we were completely loved and cherished. She left the earth a whole lot better than it was before she got here. She was always picking up stray kids or lonely senior citizens to help them out or bring them home. There were always guests without their own families with us for the holidays. She'd bring meals to the guy who lived at the dump (whom Louis also knew by the way). That counts. She was a wonderful writer and did sweet feature articles on local characters for the Greenwood Lake News. Everyone knew her and she helped everyone that she could. She was a woman involved and invested in this world.

Anyone would have been proud to be her mother. Or father.

Even Olga. Even Joe.

Olga died only about two years before my mother did. I'd like to think that they are now catching up on lost time in heaven. And if Joe Kelly is there (even with his three women friends, like the psychic said), I hope the three of them are having some sort of reckoning and figuring things out.

Finally coming to peace.

And I hope that all three of them maybe got a kick out of this book. Maybe they got a chuckle from their stories? Maybe now can hang together without shame, secrets, regrets and torment.

I sure hope so.

20

MAKING THE CASE ABOUT JOE KELLY AND OLGA MARTIN

NO DOUBT SOME OF THIS story and evidence is confusing, so it's time for a quick summary of my circumstantial evidence about Joe and Olga and how I came to the conclusion that they were my mother's parents.

- The fact that Olga and Joe lived around the corner from each other for years, including the time of my mother's conception, is my strongest evidence. New York City is a huge place. The world is a huge place. All along, putting my grandparents together was the biggest obstacle for me, and discovering them in such close proximity to one another was a miracle. The fact that Joe and Olga were city neighbors who might even have attended school together, is tremendous circumstantial evidence.

- I had ruled out the actress connection (although I will admit that there is a part of me that is still holding out hope that my conclusion is wrong and that Lucille Ball could still be my grandmother too)

- I ruled out the Jersey City Horseshoe District with the Irish railroad workers connection. Initially I thought there may have been a Kelly – Baxter railroad connection as my ungrandfather Patrick Kelly and a few of the Baxters worked on the railroad. I could not find a connection that produced my mother.

- I still wonder if the carriage house where Michael Kelly worked was the same one where both of Olga's grandfathers, Charles Crowe and Robert Martin, worked. Were the families friends?

- Finding the perfect centimorgan level for my two half-first Kelly cousins and half-aunt Mariah confirmed that Joe Kelly was, indeed, my mother's father. I am related to a lot of other Kelly cousins from the same Kelly clan in County Galway, but no where near the levels that I am related to these three. They are related to each other and the other Kelly cousins (including Hubert the family rock star).

- Creating the backwards family tree using Helen's centimorgan count as likely third cousins (which turned out to be true) was crucial to putting me on the right path investigating our great-grandparents and their siblings. Just to be careful and to account for the wide variance in centimorgan counts, I started with all of Helen's great-great-grandparents and their siblings. I went back a generation before third cousins as I didn't want to miss anyone. That process eventually led me right to Olga's

DNA door. Helen's great-grandmother Emma Crowe Martin is the sister of my great-grandfather James Crowe Martin, Olga's father.

- Although I was pretty sure I had figured out the mystery, I still felt I had to rule out all of the family stories. Erika Perallon, at the New York Foundling Hospital, researched whether or not my mother was ever one of their babies. She reported, "After an extensive search, there was no record located on the microfiche." *My mother was never at the Foundling Home.*

- Olga is the only person that I know of who genetically combines the Crowe and Koehler families. I am highly genetically connected to these people.

- I am very strongly connected genetically to Baden, Germany. Many of the Koehler and Keppler relatives come from Baden. Using Ancestry.com's Shared Location tab, I was able to confirm that dozens of my Ancestry cousins also have family from Baden.

- The MTDNA (maternal DNA lineage) test indicated that there was only one 0-degree connection in my female ancestry line, my cousin Mark. His female line went back to Suzanna Armbruster. Suzanna was also from Baden, Germany. Because the MTDNA test searches only maternal links, and because I am related to Suzanna Armbruster and Louise Koehler, Louise and Suzanna have to be related to each other. I've gotten a ton of records and still haven't figured out exactly how Suzanna and Louise are related to each other. That absolutely remains a burr in my boots. Their connection started in Baden, Germany. Louise's grandparents were both from Baden.

- Suzanna Armbruster and her husband Jacob Clouse emigrated from Baden, Germany, to a town in Sullivan County, New York only about five to seven miles from where the Grays were living. Suzanna was deceased by the time my mother was born, but a few of her children were still living in the same place.

- The towns in Sullivan County at the time of my mother's birth were tiny, and everyone knew everyone's business. Surely Suzanna and Jacob, or their kids and grandkids would have known that the Grays had adopted a baby a few years earlier. Perhaps they asked the Grays if they might want another child. Maybe the Grays seemed like a family of some means. It appears that they owned a camera, which was unusual in 1921. And the pictures show a well-dressed family.

- Jennie Gray was a local school teacher and was quite likely well respected. Were any of the Clouse children in her classes? Jennie would not have refused an offer of a second baby. It appears that the Baden, Germany Armbruster/ Clouse country cousins were maybe trying to help their Baden, Germany Koehler/Keppler/ Horkheimer/Martin city cousins with their extra baby problem. (Louise Keppler's mother's name was originally Nanette Horkheimer). All of these families were at the same place at the same time.

- The circumstantial evidence that Olga was my grandmother is strong but it is not iron-clad. I may never be able to prove it as I cannot get my mother's birth certificate. It's maddening, but it is what it is.

- And I believe what I believe – *Olga was my grandmother, and Joe was my grandfather.*

21

WHAT WAS LOST HAS BEEN FINALLY FOUND!

So, THE UNEXPECTED NUCLEAR ENDING. For me. And for you.

I thought I was finished with this book at the end of Chapter 20. It was just weeks before the book was due to go to the editor. Seemed like the end, huh. Musings belong at the end.

But ... okay. So do you remember in Chapter 3 when I mentioned that my mother had a baby she gave up for adoption? And that, as I embarked on this search for my grandparents, the person I was *really* holding out hope for, every day, was my half-sibling? And every day ... nothing. Every day they weren't on my Ancestry.com list of *Immediate Family*.

Well, on Dec. 8, 2018, I finally found her!

My sister – our sister – was finally there. Our sister Candy. She is a nurse and a pilot in North Carolina. She went to Woodstock and tried out for the Olympics. She is very groovy and brilliant.

My sister...

I knew in an instant who she was. Her centimorgan count is more than 1650. A perfect level for a half sibling. I looked at the shared matches. And, yup, she matched both the Kelly and Crowe Martin cousins. Only one person brings those two families together – our mother.

I found my sister! I finally found my sister! I had almost given up. It hit me like a lightning bolt, charging every cell in my body.

But... I didn't know if she knew she was adopted. I didn't know if she knew she might have another family. I didn't know if she even wanted to know who she was. After the terrorism allegations, I had learned to go very slowly and gently with people. I didn't want to scare anyone away and I didn't want to get arrested.

I was going to describe our initial communications but decided to transcribe it instead. I will show what I actually said *(and in parentheses and italics what I was really thinking)*.

<u>ROBIN</u>: "Hi Candace. I popped on Ancestry today *(like I do every day looking for you)* and saw that you came right up on top. Wow. You're like an early Christmas present. I always find this stuff exciting"

(What I was really thinking was, "Oh my God, Oh my God, Oh my God. I finally found you!!! You're my sister!! Oh my God!!")

"Now comes the fun part; trying to figure out how we are

connected. Do you like how I just presumed that you'd be just as curious? Ha!"

(What I was really thinking was, "Please, please respond! Please want to be my sister!" Just act cool and cavalier.)

"I can't tell which part of the family you're connected to yet; maternal or paternal side? Do you show up as more Irish? British? Or maybe a little German?"

(I was totally lying. I knew exactly who she was. I checked all of that stuff out first. I was still trying to be cool)

"I'm in New York. Anyway, it's really fun to introduce myself to you and find such a close family member. Robin Gerry"

CANDY: "Hello Robin! I am excited to see I have such a close match. I wasn't expecting much from this DNA search but a friend suggested I try it.

From the number of centimorgans we share, we may be closer than cousins."

(She knows! She knows! She knows we're sisters! Oh my God!)

"I was born in Binghamton, NY and adopted shortly after birth so I have no idea who my biological relatives may be. Perhaps you may be able to help me. I look forward to communicating with you."

ROBIN: "Hi Candace. I know your story. We've been looking for you forever!!!

My mother was from the Binghamton area. And she had given a child up for adoption.

I believe we are half sisters!!

We've been trying so hard to find you. I've been looking for you for over 25 years.

I love you already."

Pretty cool right? Damn cool right? Just writing all of that makes me cry. Every time I read this, I cry. I think it will always make me cry. It should make me cry.

Within an hour of finding her online, we were talking. We couldn't stop crying. I literally couldn't stop crying. That had never in my life happened before. They were tears of happiness, tears of joy, tears of wonder.

And I think maybe they were the tears of generations of pain and trauma that seeped into my DNA from all of my traumatized ancestors? People who had endured the horror of immigration, intense poverty, loss of children and spouses, the loss of family and country.

Can it work like that? Can we really cry the tears of our ancestors?

Tears of joy and resolution. Finally feeling the family together and complete? Can we really cry our ancestors' tears? Oh God, yes!

I just couldn't believe we finally found her.

Candy was soaking everything up about our mother – her mother. I sent her pictures and told her all I could think to tell her. I am sure she was overwhelmed. She's now on a sister text thread with my other two sisters, and we all are loving it. There are already a gazillion texts and pictures flying back and forth. We communicate almost every day.

Talking to Candy about our mother has actually brought Dawn, Billie and me closer. I think it's because talking about Mom makes her seem nearer to all four of us now and helps us remember and feel our mother. What a Christmas blessing for all of us!

For Christmas, our sister Dawn gifted Candy with a promise that every day for a year she would share a memory, picture, story or quirk about our mother so Candy could begin to get a sense of who her mom was. Isn't that a spectacular gift? We will all get to share that sacred sister bonding.

Naturally there were questions. What happened? Why was Candy given up? Who was her father? Things that our very secretive mother likely never told anyone.

It was about twenty-five years ago, after our mother had died, my father casually mentioned that we had a half sibling, but he didn't really know anything more than that.

I believed him and then wrote to my uncle Donald to find out what he knew about my sibling. I didn't even consider the possibility that he wouldn't answer my questions truthfully.

It took a while, but he finally acknowledged that there had been a baby who had maybe been born in Nevada. But he didn't know the year of birth or the baby's gender. Talk about an impossible wild goose chase.

Uncle Donald also wrote that our mother had had an affair with her married boss who worked in the automobile industry. That part turned out to be true.

We now know that our mother had a baby girl. And she set the baby free for adoption directly from the hospital. She never took her baby home. I am sure she knew if she had taken the baby home, even for a nano-second, she would have fallen in love with her.

After we found Candy and did the math, we realized that our uncle and our mother had actually been living in the same town at the time, and she delivered Candy at a nearby hospital. He had been right there. He had to have known. He was married at the time, so I assume my aunt knew, too. It all occurred while Jennie Butler Gray was dying. Jennie died a little less than nine months after Candy was born. Our mother lost her mother and a daughter within nine months. How painful must all of that have been? To further complicate things, our aunt gave birth to our cousin around the same time. More trauma for our mother, blessings for the rest of the family.

Initially I was really upset with Uncle Donald for being untruthful. It never entered my brain that he might not be forthcoming. Why was that? Why hadn't I even considered that possibility? Maybe I was just naive.

Then I tried to think about why he would still cover up a pregnancy that occurred thirty-something years before my request and after his sister had died, especially knowing first-hand the pain of adoption and having been aware of my mother's adoption pain as well.

How could he interfere with siblings trying to find each other, and not help another orphan? All I could come up with is that he was still trying to protect his sister, even after her death. How could anyone fault him for that? It's honestly touching, although it would be more touching if I weren't involved. But I am touched by my uncle's devotion to his adopted sister. Forever.

My mother had named the baby Donna Gray. Was Donna Gray named after her brother Donald Gray? The thing I struggle to get beyond, though, is how she could she do the same thing to her baby knowing how painful and devastating it was for her? I guess we all have a tendency to re-create out childhood traumas to try to triumph over them?

I know what it was like for me to finally look upon the faces of my grandparents. It was almost like being able to stop a dream from slipping away, kind of like freezing time. I can't even imagine what it was like for Candy to look upon the face of her mother and sisters after spending a lifetime wishing and wondering. How does one describe something like that? I guess we would need an adopted poet to tell us that. I don't have the words to express something so big. It's like trying to describe the greens of Ireland or Native American petroglyphs in ancient caves. Sometimes there are just no words, only indescribable feelings. Sacred feelings. Primal feelings.

Like us, Candy was surprised and happy to learn that she was pretty darn Irish and a bit of German. She had always suspected it, but she loved knowing a specific place that her family came from: Menlough, Vermount, County Galway, Ireland. She had dark auburn hair and green eyes. Our mother's hair was auburn but her eyes were blue. My sisters and I – with the exception of Candy – have blue eyes. Candy certainly looks more like her father.

In her joy over finding us and being immediately accepted and loved by us, she described it as, "This fills the hole I've had in my heart."

There it is again.

Heart hole.

The exact same thing our mother said to me all those decades ago. I was stunned. I assume this is a universal feeling, but I can't help but wonder if Candy's heart hole was all hers? Or was our mother able to transmit part of her own heart hole to all four of her daughters? Was Candy's heart hole amplified because of her own adoption?

Candy's story gets better. Just seven days after she found her biological mother, she found her biological father. Lightning struck twice in a week for her. I'm not going to say much about her father or what all that was about because it's not my story. But I will say that Candy learned she has four more half siblings. Crazy, right? She went from no siblings to seven siblings in just one week. Talk about a wild ride.

Naturally, she was on the text thread with all of us as this was going on and she was making first contact with her paternal siblings. Billie and Dawn and I got to witness her miracle in real time. What a soul rushing honor for us.

Witnessing her miracle unfold gave me both an involved, yet separate perspective. I found myself hoping and praying she would find her answers, find her peace. She was a woman I had never even heard of until a week ago, yet I found myself wrapped up in a desperate hope that she wouldn't be hurt and rejected by her new paternal family, that she would be accepted by this other new family.

I was feeling protective of her. Already. I was stunned that her quest was somehow becoming my hope. Is that even normal? I can't really describe my feelings. Maybe it was a primal sort of thing. How could I feel so bonded to such a new person?

Is there an intergenerational, historical, family cosmic cord that supersedes life and time? Are families really connected to each other forever? Boy, do I hope so.

This was all happening a couple of weeks before Christmas, a really sacred, mystical time. Is the shroud between past and present, really more accessible at this time of year? It sure seems so. Were Olga and our mother helping to amp up Candy's quest into light speed? Were they helping the second and – hopefully! – final orphan in this family find her peace? It sure felt like that.

We all finally met and hung out together in Florida. All of us were stunned at how easy and instantly we bonded. Our sister Dawn kept saying it felt more like we just hadn't seen her for a while; not that we didn't know her. I had read all of the cautionary posts about keeping first contact expectations low and was prepared to be polite and congenial. For us it was unnecessary. We all just love her so much already. Candy herself reminded us of the song 'We are Family. I got all my sisters with me' by Sister Sledge. Proof of the bonding is that we even wound up having a sister misunderstanding. Sisters! We got that out of the way.

We all had the feeling that our mother would have been happy and at peace to finally have all of her daughters together. We were blubby messes at the airport when we had to break up the sisterhood. And that's ok. It's human. We promised to do it at least once a year.

What a soul bending journey this has been for me. I started out trying to find our sibling and thought I got shut down by the adoptive family, so out of respect I purposely let it drop and instead focused on finding my elusive grandparents. I found them and was ready to put a bow on the end of the story and ... BAM! Here comes our sister. You just can't make this stuff up. It was all perfectly timed. Again, the finger of God was all over this quest.

I don't know why I should have been so blessed with all of these blessings, but I was. And I will work forever to honor it and try to pay it forward. I am so very lucky and grateful.

We found our sister......

Left to right: Dawn Mazur, Candy Carter, Billie 'Boo' Manes and Robin
We are all wearing the same scarves from Ireland.

22

TRANSFORMING

THIS QUEST HAS BLOWN EVERYTHING apart. My sense of who I am. Where I come from. Who my people are. How this strange story of an illegal baby hand-off nearly one hundred years ago utterly and completely impacted and blasted through every cell in my body.

I never knew.

I never understood.

Heck, I never even thought about it.

I am writing this final chapter on the same day I voted in the 2018 U.S. mid-term elections.

This was the first time I've seen the voting hall jam-packed. No parking, huge turn-out, multi-cultural people waiting patiently to vote. It was the first time I really thought about the ancestors who gave their lives to allow me to vote my heart and speak my mind. I never thought about voting like that before.

I was reminded of the sweet Irish farmer, Jack, who spoke about the Kellys (and the Gavins, Ruanes, Potters etc) who fought and died for Irish independence as we stood before the Menlough, Ireland war memorial. I was remembering the history of the Kelly kings of Ireland who fought to save their country from the invading Vikings. And the other Kellys who died in WWI and WWII trying to stop Nazis and fascists. My German ancestors fleeing the aftermath of the Napoleanic war carnage and devastation.

And, of course, my parents' military service.

Would I be thinking so historically, so "ancestrally" had I not just come through this soul rocking process? I feel that I wouldn't. I've voted dozens of time and never felt moved – never felt history before. It means something different to me now. Very different. I'm very different.

Thank God.

There's a field of research called epigenetics. The theory is that some traumas are so intense that they may actually change and activate genome markers that will be passed on to future generations. Change the DNA. Theoretically, it's a biological way to protect and warn our future relatives of dire danger. Can it work the other way, too? Can we pass on reverence? Gratitude? Can we touch the ancestors with our souls? And meet and thank them in dreams? Through feelings? Do they walk with us? Do we dance with them? What if families don't really ever become separated? Can we learn to see them? And feel them? Hear them? Are they still trying to guide us?

True story. When my son Zack was an infant, the doctors thought he had a brain tumor and scheduled an MRI to get a look at his brain. Before getting to the MRI technician, I had spoken with the doctor and nurse who had sedated this fifteen-pound baby. They referred to his condition as "being asleep." I saw it as "being unconscious."

Anyway, as I walked him over to put him in the MRI machine, I heard a very loud, female voice say, "Tell them he has tubes in his ears." Twice. I looked over my right shoulder. No one was there. I looked over my left shoulder. No one. The voice was as clear as any voice I'd ever heard. For real.

The MRI technician even asked what I was doing. "You know he has tubes in his ears, right?" "What?! What kind of tubes? Are they metal tubes?"

I didn't know. The machine was immediately turned off and the tech called the ear, nose and throat doctor. There were, indeed, metal tubes in his little ears. If that baby had gone into the MRI, the tubes would have blown out through his ear drums. He would have either become deaf or had lifelong hearing issues.

I know I sound a little looney, but it really did happen just as I described.

Who did I hear? Was that my mother? Grandmother? Is that how the worlds of the living and the deceased sometimes blend? Is that how angels work? Are the guardian angels really our ancestors still protecting us? Do they sometimes come to us through dreams or intuition? Or through mediums? Who the heck knows? I'd sure like to think they do, though. I am very comforted by the thought that the ancestors still walk with us and that someday I can keep walking with them to protect my own kids and grandkids. It is a soothing thought to me that the thread that ties families together may tie us together forever.

I am writing this chapter in a bar at the South Street Seaport in New York City, looking over the East River. I am watching Brooklyn and the Brooklyn Bridge sparkle. Naturally, I'm sipping an Irish Whiskey.

I was listening to Christmas carols on the way down to New York. Before I left, I had just stopped at a store for cat food and saw them on sale and grabbed two holiday CD's. I have always loved Christmas carols, the old ones. Particularly the spiritual ones. I always tell my kids that if I'm ever in a coma and they can't decide whether or not to pull the plug, have the doctors play Christmas carols. If I don't react and don't respond, then they have my permission to pull the plug because I will surely be gone.

The mystical, magical quality of those songs and the Christmas story always make me feel that the shroud between now and the past, dead and alive, is a little more porous and transparent during the holidays. Almost like the two worlds can touch for an instant. Almost like the two worlds are really only one world? Somehow? I think they always are just one world.

The *Auld Lang Syne* song seriously resonated with me this time. I had never paid much attention to the words before. There's a chorus that goes:

We two have paddled in the stream

From morning sun till dine;

But seas between us broad have roared

Since Auld Lang Syne

How could I hear that song now and not think of all of my Irish,

British and German ancestors who sacrificed so much to immigrate to this country? How they became lost to each other. Lost to my parents. Lost to me and all of my sisters. The trauma and sorrow of immigration and broken family ties and broken lives seemed to resonate in every cell in my body.

I found myself thinking about Olga. Crying. Crying for her sad sacrifice and horrible soul-breaking loss. Happy, though, that she will be remembered now. Who else was missing her? Crying for her? This book for me, is like lighting a candle for her. And my mother. And the Kelly babies Winifred and Michael. And poor Frederick Koehler who died so young. And even Joe Kelly.

All of them. Every one of them.

I was crying for my mother's lifelong pain and longing for her mother. And my mom's longing for her own lost daughter.

And I was crying for my sisters and myself, never knowing our grandparents and that family line and unwittingly absorbing our mother's raw, brutal emotional wounds.

I can never again hear *Auld Lang Syne* without becoming teary and without thinking about Olga and our mother. And even Joe.

I'm waiting for Louis to finish up with his business to meet me.

Louis...

None of this would have happened without him. The man who always walks with his own ancestors. What made him teach me how to finally find and feel my missing family? How did we even find each other in the first place? Maybe it's the whiskey, but I found myself wondering if maybe we both were being led by the ones who've passed. Do they still influence us? Have they always been there?

Louis finally showed up. He had an Irish whiskey, too, and we had a toast to the ancestors.

I read him what I had just written. We both got a little teary. Teary at the magnitude of what we had accomplished. Teary at what we now know about how much trauma and sorrow my people went through and survived. Teary about how close the ancestors felt that night. How this quest brought us together and stopped each of us from being solitary emotional vagabonds. Our cups runneth over. How lucky and blessed are we?

A young man walked by and told us he thought we were cute together. Cute? We are a thousand years old. That was weird but sweet. What was drawing him toward us? He later came by again with his niece and wanted to buy us a drink. Louis did his avuncular thing with the young man, and I talked with the fifteen-year-old niece (Admittedly I felt uncomfortable that she was even in a bar), who was in distress because people on the streets had just been telling her to go back to her own country. She was Native American and Colombian. This is her country! I talked to her about how stunningly beautiful she was to be the face of two such magnificent cultures. She really was gorgeous. She talked to me about how loving Columbian people are to each other and how proud she is of her heritages. Bravo to her. Bravo that she knows who her people are and what their story was. She might have tricky parts to her life, but certainly not a heart hole.

Louis and I left and headed back to his apartment. On the way home I was texting my new cousin Colleen Kelly and sending her pics of the city lights. She's in Denver, Colorado. I love her.

Louis had a surprise. He had bought a new music system. He had *John Denver's "Rocky Mountain High"* ready to play as the first song. It was certainly a Rocky Mountain High night between Colleen and the music.

That has always been one of my top three favorite songs, ever. We danced to it and sang it to each other. Two times.

And I know we aren't dancing alone. This time I know that it was an Irish, German, English and Italian jamboree!

My heart is now lighter and fuller. I can sing and dance again.

EPILOGUE

Throughout this journey, this totally unexpected, mystical soul journey, my two adult sons, Max and Zack, have been in the background. When I tried to talk to them about my discoveries of the family – their family, too, they would give each other the side-eye stink-eye. Then they'd glaze over and do that polite stare right at me, right through me, while they devised ways to escape hearing what I was spouting.

On the rare occasion that they asked a question about what I was so absorbed in, I could see they were just trying to be kind. Their girlfriends asked me more than they ever did.

At one point, when I was discouraged, one of them even tried to encourage me, "Oh, don't worry about it. It doesn't matter. All those people are dead, anyway. Besides, you have us."

Oh good grief. That sure sounds familiar.

Another future ancestor quest begins?

And a heart hole finally closes!

The author's sons; Max Gaydos (left) and Zack Gaydos (right). They are in front of the old, decrepit bed frame with the Kelly loo rock just above Max's left ear. The other rocks are from the sacred Native American cave in Oregon

They are unaware that their soul quest has begun...

ABOUT THE AUTHOR

Robin Gerry is an artist and a mother. She currently works in a children's trauma and abuse unit in Orange County, NY as part of a team comprised of professionals from the District Attorney's office, the County Attorney's office, Child Protective Services, Law Enforcement and Mental Health. The team works with children and families who are victims of felony crimes including murder, rape, sexual and physical assault.

She is also the Co-Chair of the Trauma Institute of Orange County. She provides trainings in working with childhood sexual assault and trauma, vicarious trauma etc.

It is through understanding the impact of historical and familial trauma in her work, that she was able to finally piece her own family story together and understand the impact of the inter-generational trauma in her own family.

For additional copies of this book or to arrange a book signing, contact Robin at robinmgerry@gmail.com or Healing the Family Heart Holes on FaceBook. The book is also available at Amazon.com

JAMES KELLY
NANCY CARROL
FRED KOEHLER
LOUISE
ADAM KEPPLER
NANETTE
PATRICK KELLY
WINIFRED GAVIN
FREDERICK KOEHLER
LOUISE KEPPLER
JOHANNA RITTINGER
CHARLES CROWE
JAMES DOWLING
MAE McGUIRE
JAMES CROWE MARTIN
LOUISE KOEHLER
MICHAEL KELLY
MARIA DOWLING
OLGA MARTIN
JOE KELLY
BARBARA KATHERINE GRAY

Made in the USA
Middletown, DE
28 April 2019